LARRY & Wendy Dilley

DIANETICS 55!

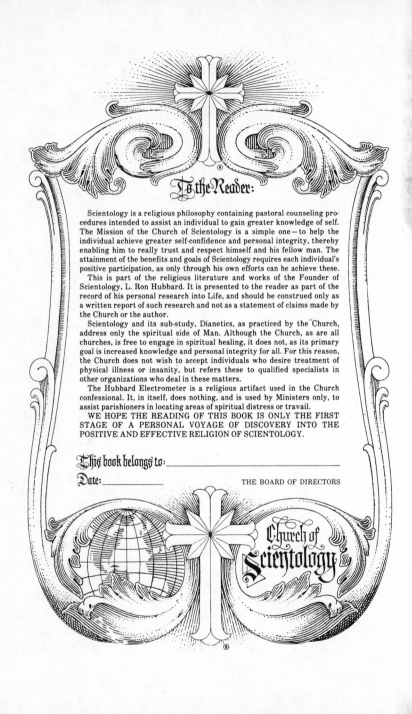

To the Reader:

Scientology is a religious philosophy containing pastoral counseling procedures intended to assist an individual to gain greater knowledge of self. The Mission of the Church of Scientology is a simple one—to help the individual achieve greater self-confidence and personal integrity, thereby enabling him to really trust and respect himself and his fellow man. The attainment of the benefits and goals of Scientology requires each individual's positive participation, as only through his own efforts can he achieve these.

This is part of the religious literature and works of the Founder of Scientology, L. Ron Hubbard. It is presented to the reader as part of the record of his personal research into Life, and should be construed only as a written report of such research and not as a statement of claims made by the Church or the author.

Scientology and its sub-study, Dianetics, as practiced by the Church, address only the spiritual side of Man. Although the Church, as are all churches, is free to engage in spiritual healing, it does not, as its primary goal is increased knowledge and personal integrity for all. For this reason, the Church does not wish to accept individuals who desire treatment of physical illness or insanity, but refers these to qualified specialists in other organizations who deal in these matters.

The Hubbard Electrometer is a religious artifact used in the Church confessional. It, in itself, does nothing, and is used by Ministers only, to assist parishioners in locating areas of spiritual distress or travail.

WE HOPE THE READING OF THIS BOOK IS ONLY THE FIRST STAGE OF A PERSONAL VOYAGE OF DISCOVERY INTO THE POSITIVE AND EFFECTIVE RELIGION OF SCIENTOLOGY.

This book belongs to: _____

Date: _____   THE BOARD OF DIRECTORS

Church of Scientology

DIANETICS® 55!

by

L. RON HUBBARD

PUBLICATIONS ORGANIZATION
UNITED STATES

Published by

Church of Scientology of California
Publications Organization
4833 Fountain Avenue, East Annex
Los Angeles, California 90029

Scientology is an applied religious philosophy.

Dianetics® and Scientology® are registered names.

The Church of Scientology of California is a non profit organization.

Tenth Edition, July 1974

REPRINTED DECEMBER 1975
REPRINTED MARCH 1976
REPRINTED AUGUST 1976
REVISED EDITION OCTOBER 1979

A Dianetics® Publication

Dianetics is the trademark of
L. Ron Hubbard in respect of
his published works.

ISBN 0-88404-003-8

Printed in the United States of America

CONTENTS

Important Note

In studying Dianetics and Scientology be very, very certain you never go past a word you do not fully understand.

The only reason a person gives up a study or becomes confused or unable to learn is that he or she has gone past a word or phrase that was not understood.

Trying to read past a misunderstood word results in mental "fogginess" and difficulty in comprehending the passages which follow. If you find yourself experiencing this, return to the last portion you understood easily, locate the misunderstood word and get it defined correctly —and then go on.

Most of the terms used in this book are defined as they occur. For additional definitions see the Glossary starting on page 171.

FOREWORD

SECRET! Secrets, secrets, SECRETS! Ah, the endless quest, the far, far search, the codes, the vias, the symbols, the complications, the compilations, the mathematicity and abstractacity of secrets, secrets, secrets.

And truth. TRUTH! From Keats to Johnny Jones, we all have traffic with the truth, truth, TRUTH! The professors have a truth, the religionists have a truth, the stars and almost anything but government have a truth, truth, TRUTH.

Knowledge! Endeared as a precious torch, abhorred as a neurotic's nightmare, it is all knowledge, knowledge, Knowledge! You get diplomas for it and buy books full of it, you perish for the lack of it or triumph in the absence of it, but whatever it might be, knowledge is precious, dangerous, valueless and horrible and craved.

And what is knowledge? And what is the SECRET? and what is TRUTH?

Pontius Pilate asked the question when he washed his hands. Alexander executed messengers when the Truth was unpalatable. The Chaldean priest corralled a bit of truth and ruled Chaldea into yesterday and Babylon into dust motes. And rulers and men, scholars and generals have condemned with it, dedicated their lives to it, fought for it and denied it and—have never defined it.

What is TRUTH? What is KNOWLEDGE? What is the SECRET? Are they inventions from a shaman's dream? Are they connected with science? Do they belong to philosophy? What are they, whence do they come? Do they exist? Are they owned? Have they ever been written or spoken or guessed? And would one go mad if he knew them?

Dianetics moved into the world on May 9, 1950, with the publication of a book, DIANETICS: THE MODERN SCIENCE OF MENTAL HEALTH. It moved with violence although its message was peace. A half a million Americans read it, many, many of these acted upon it and are still acting upon it, and every year it sells still more copies—more copies than the average "best seller."

Dianetics was an adventure into the dark realms of the secret to accumulate knowledge and to establish the truth. Until Dianetics these commodities have been owned by philosophy of either the esoteric or the monotony schools or had been used by the charlatan—with or without surplice—to lure and ensnare.

Dianetics moved into a Dark Age of Reason where only a physical universe fact was given credence. When Dianetics was born every free thinker Man had known had long since been burned or poisoned or dust-binned into the curriculums of "universities." It was an age where renown awaited only the manufacturer — not the inventor — of the new can opener, where sanity was adjusted with electrodes and philosophy was made with Univacs. Knowledge and the SECRET being the total assets of vested interest, Dianetics was hit with violence from many quarters. Medicine, entirely cognizant that it could not cure nor even alleviate the majority of Man's ills, yet like a prima donna who can but croak yet resists the incoming next act, bluntly and viciously condemned in leading weekly magazines, any further glance towards knowledge and truth. The government, fighting a war at the time, entirely cognizant that its pilot supply was old and slow, yet could not communicate on any subject which might remedy the matter. The Better Business Bureaus of the U.S., an organization solidly behind anything good and solid, upheld the objection of capital to this new idea; the Communist Party, being solidly against any alteration of the mind since that would undoubtedly alter devotion, went to considerable lengths to assist the stand of capital. To anyone who wanted a monopoly on knowledge and truth Dianetics was an enemy. To them it was a degraded, wicked, fraudulent hoax—or so they said. However, there happens to be a principle that anything which is thoroughly understood ceases. Their opinion of Dianetics could not have been correct because Dianetics is still here.

During the ensuing four years of commotion, much happened. The only orderly and progressive thing which happened was that Dianetics went on encroaching into the territory of the SECRET along the roadway of KNOWLEDGE to discover nearer TRUTH.

The primary assault of Dianetics was upon reverence and forms. The first book was written as a javelin directed into the doubtlessly sacrosanct vitals of philosophical departments and literature. It was carefully careless with its commas in the belief that commas, contrary to the prevailing mode, have little power to disturb an ultimate truth. The first book was written to be read and understood, and it was written to upset and override and warn off those who would give it the fate of being reverable. And the first book was written to be used by anyone who could understand it—and the way it was written, this of course could not include the extant mental charlatan nor the professional dabbler in abilities. As one had learned these could not be trained and if they could have been, wouldn't have been interested in the proposed goals, it was necessary that a new breed of feline come into being— the auditor—and the auditor did.

Now this adventure along the road of knowledge towards truth was very shiny new in 1950. It was not quite so new but much shinier in 1954. Certain promises were made in 1950 on page 401. And these promises have now been kept.

Man *can* be cleared. He can be cleared—brought to the condition described in Chapter Two of the first book—by a well-studied and competent auditor in a relatively short length of time.

This book contains processes which were the forerunners of the clearing processes in use today. This means that auditors do have to be trained—we have found definitely that they do. It also means that an auditor who has been trained and processed can now take these newer processes and run them as directed and can achieve the result of Clear.

Thus, in DIANETICS 55! we have, actually, the SECOND BOOK of Dianetics. Everyone has assigned the title First Book to DIANETICS: THE MODERN SCIENCE OF MENTAL HEALTH. But nobody has ever referred to SCIENCE OF SURVIVAL, published in 1951, as the Second Book. They haven't because it obviously wasn't. SCIENCE OF SURVIVAL was a first book in its own right.

It was the first book of and under Plan C on page 401 of the real First Book. SCIENCE OF SURVIVAL adventured into causation, not into the resolution of problems outlined in the First Book.

Thus there has never been a Second Book of Dianetics. Such a book would have to take the exact problems of the First Book and in the terms and reference of the First Book resolve these problems.

Well, as one looks over fiction novels and technical volumes in general he finds that a four year—almost five— lag between an author's first and second volume would discover his public to have waned. But when we take up a subject of the status of Dianetics and when we realize that it is condensing into a few years some thousands of years of doing, we see that a lag of four or five years between volumes isn't so very bad.

What happened in those four or five years? Many things. Somehow, for one thing, research and development was financed and the basic organization, after many limpings, survived. A lot of petty things happened which in another decade will be bone dust—for none of these things, none of the tales of terror, the attacks, the financing, the business advances, were permitted to interrupt the only thing that CAN mean any difference—the product of years of steady gain on the road of knowledge towards the goal of ultimate truth.

Knowledge, Truth, Secrets—they are the guts and anatomy of life. They must not then be owned. They must not then be hidden or bent. They must be permitted to stand out in the bold sunlight for all to see for only when they are to be seen are they safe things to have, to hold, to know.

This is the Second Book of Dianetics. It *could* mean a new Earth, it could mean a new freedom. But whatever it means it cannot mean *nothing* in the sense Man uses that word—for you cannot unveil the SECRET and have it ever be quite so secret ever again.

L. Ron Hubbard
Phoenix, 1954

NOTE : Much of what in this book was termed Dianetics is, in today's technical lineup, *Scientology* technology. The two fields are as follows :

> DIANETICS®: From the Greek *dia* (through) and *noos* (soul), thus "through the soul"; a system for the analysis, control and development of human thought which also provides techniques for increased ability, rationality, and freedom from the discovered single source of aberrations and psychosomatic ills. Introduced May, 1950, with publication of *Dianetics: The Modern Science of Mental Health* by L. Ron Hubbard.

> SCIENTOLOGY® is an applied religious philosophy and technology resolving problems of the spirit, life and thought; discovered, developed and organized by L. Ron Hubbard as a result of his earlier Dianetic discoveries. Coming from the Latin, *scio* (knowing) and the Greek *logos* (study), Scientology means "knowing how to know" or "the study of wisdom."

CHAPTER I

DIANETICS

Why should anyone want to know anything about the human mind? And, for that matter, why should anyone believe that knowledge of the human mind is either unobtainable or undesirable? Why should men ostensibly seeking answers to the mind stray so far from it as to examine rats and entirely avoid looking at human beings? And why should anyone pretending to treat the mind stray so far afield as electric shock?

The answers are relatively simple. Anyone who knows the structure, function, and dynamics of the human mind is very difficult to control. The only way a mind can be controlled is by enforcing upon it ignorance of itself. As far as study and treatment is concerned, a mind which has been made ignorant of itself would have to have restored to it awareness of its fundamentals before it could be considered to be recovered. And when one restores full awareness to a mind one is no longer able to victimize it. And a profession or a society would have to move out of slave orientation into action by freedom and consent, were it to be effective.

Just as you do not want people to control you, so you should want knowledge of yourself and others. Just as you fight away from knowingness concerning self, so you will be controlled.

A simple and conclusive science of mind is a vital necessity in any society which desires to become free and remain free. The only elements in a society which would combat, or contest, or dispute an effort to attain such a science would be those interests which desired, by ignorance, to maintain their control of a slavery. Each and every impulse of freedom is an impulse towards sanity, towards health, towards happiness. Every impulse towards slavery is an impulse in the direction of misery, disease and death. One can say alike of the arthritic and the neurotic that the basic cause of disturbance, physical or mental, germinated in efforts to reduce the freedom of the individual, the group, or Mankind.

Dianetics is an effort towards the attainment by Man of a level of freedom where decency and happiness can prevail, and where knowledge of the mind itself would prevent the unscrupulous use of the mechanisms of slavery. Dianetics can be contested, it can be vilified, its founder and practitioners can be publicly pilloried, but Dianetics cannot be ignored. It could neither be drowned in praise, nor burned in some purge to its total eradication, for it is a wonderfully observable fact that the one impulse in Man which cannot be erased is his impulse towards freedom, his impulse towards sanity, towards higher levels of attainment in all of his endeavours. This is Man's one saving grace, and because Dianetics is such an impulse, and because its basic purpose, from the moment of its conception, have been dedicated unswervably to the attainment of even greater freedom it cannot perish—a fact which will become doubtlessly more annoying to the slave-masters as the years roll on.

There is much argument upon which we could adventure concerning whether Dianetics is an art or a science, whether it is a humanity or a hoax, but all this would avail us very little for we would only be quibbling with words. Dianetics is what it is, and the totality of it can best be summed by the description, 'an understanding of Man.' We do not care whether or not it is a science. We do not care whether or not it is more properly catalogued under Adventure or Mystery. We do care whether or not it is promulgated and known, for everywhere it walks slavery ceases. That mind which understands itself is the mind of a free man. It is no longer prone to obsessive behaviour, unthinking compliances, covert innuendoes. It is at home in an environment, not a stranger. It is the solver of problems and the maker of games. A mind that is enslaved is weak. A mind that is free is powerful, and all the power there is, is defined by and contained in freedom.

Why should you know something about your mind? A question of a similar magnitude would be: "Why should you live?" A science fiction writer once conceived a world composed entirely of machines, composed to a point where the machines were repaired by other machines, which, in turn, were repaired by yet other machines, and so the circle went 'round and the machines survived. He wrote this story from the fondest belief of nuclear physicists that there is only a machine, that man derives from some spontaneous combustion of mud, that the soul does not exist, that freedom is impossible, that all behaviour is stimulus-response, that causative thought cannot exist. What a world this would be! And yet this world, this pattern, is the goal of the slavemakers. If every man could be depressed from his freedom to a point where he believed himself but a cog in an enormous machine, then all things would be enslaved. But who would there be to enjoy them? Who would there be to profit? Not the slavemaker, for he is the first to succumb. He succumbs to his own mechanisms. He receives the full jolt of his own endeavours to entrap. What would be the purpose of this world of machines? There could be no purpose worth contemplating which does not include happiness and experience. When a man is no longer able to envision happiness as a part of his future, that man is dead. He has become nothing but an animated robot, without understanding, without humanity, perfectly willing then to compose missiles of such detonative quality that an entire civilization can perish, and that the happiness of all can be destroyed in the experience of radiation—an experience which might be considered digestible by an atomic pile, but not by a human being. Thus as we depart from the concepts of freedom, we depart into a darkness where the will, the fear, or the brutality, of one or a few, no matter how well educated, may yet obliterate everything for which we have worked, everything for which we have hoped. This is what happens when the machine runs wild, and when Man, become a machine, runs wild. Man can only become a machine when he is no longer capable of understanding his own beingness and has lost his contact with it. Thus it is of enormous importance that we understand something about the mind, that we understand we are minds, that we are not machines, and it is of enormous importance that Man attain at once to some higher level of freedom where the machine reaction of destruction may be controlled, and where Man himself can enjoy some of the happiness to which he is entitled.

"Dianetics: The Modern Science of Mental Health" was written into a world where atomic fission was yet in its early stages. But "Dianetics 55!" is being written in a world where bombs exist of such fury that a continent could be laid waste. The recent declaration of the Secretary of War of the United States of America that such weapons exist, and are capable of being used, and his assumption that men exist with such insufficiency of humanity that they would use such weapons, tells us that it is time someone, somewhere, took a hand in this game. The intimacy of his promises cannot be escaped. You would think anyone a madman who essayed to destroy every book in every library in the United States and Russia. You would think a man quite insane if he insisted upon the destruction of all your personal possessions. You would know he was mad when he insisted that the only course for the future was the destruction of your body and any future race to remember it. Only a raving, drooling madman could contemplate the ending of all goals everywhere on earth. And only an apathetic fool would stand by motionless before the inevitable destruction of his most intimate dreams, his fondest hopes, his possessions—even on down to his identification cards and the money in his wallet. Such destruction permits no inheritance. It means an end of everything for which we have all hoped, for which we and our ancestors have striven, and it is my belief that an individual who can contemplate this with equanimity and without an impulse to act is so lost to the race and lost to himself, to his family, and to his friends, that he must personally believe there is no hope for anything, anywhere, at any time. Such depravity is difficult to envision. We know, definitely, that the wrong thing to do is nothing. Whenever any situation may develop, we always have that answer. It is wrong to do nothing. The only time anyone has ever gotten into serious trouble was when he decided he could do nothing about something.

This was the entering threshold towards death. When one *knew*, at last, that he was powerless in the face of all fates, or of any one particular fate, he was, to that degree, a slave of those fates. Thus, the wrong thing to do in this world, at this time, is nothing. No matter what fantastic or incredible plan we adventure upon, no matter how we put it forward, it would still be better than the abandonment of all plans and all action. It may be that we have better plans than fantastic plans. It may be that we, possessed of a knowledge of the mind and of Man, can yet restrain this dreadful crime of oblivion from occurring.

Dianetics, then, is a weapon. It is a timely weapon. It is the only weapon of defence in existence which can confront with equanimity nuclear fission. Dianetics can fail only if it is not used, only if those who know about it do not use it to its fullest extent. Were you to take the technologies of Dianetics this day, and seeking out anyone even remotely connected with the responsibility for waging atomic war, apply these techniques to them, you would soon have the man into a sufficiently high stratum of humanity that he would recognize some of his responsibility to the human race. Your task would be made hard, for all those who are connected with the waging of war with atomic fission are restricted by law from receiving any psychotherapy. If this seems incredible to you, you should realize that anyone in a top-secret or confidential classification in government is not supposed to impart any information of his calling. And it is the fear of governments that some of this information might be imparted to someone practising in the field of mental healing. And thus, if anyone connected with nuclear fission is discovered to be undergoing processing of any kind, he would be immediately relieved of his post and his top-secret classification would be cancelled. But this is not a hopeless picture. Supposing one processed them all and had all their top-secret classifications cancelled, who would be left? Or supposing one pointed out this idiocy with sufficient conviction to those in charge of (but who are not responsible for) the destinies of Man, and made it mandatory that the sanity of anyone connected with the creation or use of atomic fission be required to have a sanity passport. Only the insane will destroy. Remember that! Only the insane would bring about the end of earth. One of these men, fumbling forward, uncomprehending, a mere machine, given processing begins to realize that he is not without responsibility for the safety of humanity. Only when he is a slave could he be forced to use such weapons against mankind. There is no argument on earth of sufficient emergency or violence to require war, much less war by atomic fission with the consequence of the destruction of at least one continent, and within a few years, the destruction of the planet earth.

Who would believe that anyone could wipe a continent clean of life without at once so polluting the atmosphere of earth as to endanger or eradicate all further life-forms on this planet? What argument could there be amongst men which could occasion such a fate for earth? There is no such argument amongst men. Such an argument could arise amongst machines which, conscientiously, might push buttons, reach conclusions for which they had no responsibility.

There are many ways in which a higher state of security could be attained for earth. None of these ways include violence or revolution, and all of them include a greater freedom for Mankind. Dianetics is the key technology necessary for the control of atomic fission. Remember that, and remember also that Dianetics is a precision science, that it works only when it is used as a precision science. For if you are to accomplish anything with it, whether the rescue of a relative from the pain of continued psychosomatic illness, of a group, a nation, or a world, it works exactly along the lines it is designed. It does not work with innovations. It is a precision science. It has a precision mission. It contains more answers than Man has ever had before, and it contains enough answers to make Man free—if it is used!

CHAPTER II

THE FUNDAMENTALS OF LIFE

Much more broadly covered in Scientology, the fundamentals of life yet differ in no way for Man.

The basic subdivision in life is between ability and mechanics. This could also be described as a subdivision of quality and quantity, but less accurately.

Where mechanics have ability, the ability is only apparent and has been endowed into the mechanics by life. It is all right to suppose that an electronic brain is capable of thought as long as one realizes that life itself must necessarily be present in order to give cause, and quality, or direction, to such a brain. An electronic brain will sit all day and do nothing unless life starts the machine running. It will give millions of answers, but none of these, no matter how sharp, have any meaning until they are viewed by life. The machine is never anything more than a servo-mechanism to life. Indeed, a machine cannot even exist in the absence of life.

By mechanics we mean any and all of the objects, motions, or spaces which exist. Foremost of these, and foremost in any mechanical scheme, is space. Next is energy. Next is condensed or solidified energy, called matter. And finally, always present in any mechanical arrangement or mechanic, that relative change of position of particles or objects known as time. Thus we have space, energy, matter, and time. Whether

we are considering a body running on any energy, an
automobile or a mountain, we are still dealing with what we
call here mechanics. Mechanics are always quantitative.
There is always just so much distance, or so much mass, or
so many hours. The quality of space, energy, matter, and
time has value only when viewed, used, or monitored by life,
and, indeed, cannot exist in the absence of life. Correct or
not, this is workable and is our primary assumption. We have
a word for mechanics compounded from matter, energy,
space, and time which is MEST. By MEST we mean any or
all arrangements of energy of whatever kind, whether in
fluid or object form, in space or spaces. We do not conceive
life to have an energy, and therefore, any energy, even if
directly produced by life, can be found to be embraced under
the quantitative term "MEST."

Life itself has quality and ability. The products of quality
and ability are mechanics. Ability is demonstrated by the
handling of matter, energy, space and time. Quality means
simply "valued," or "having a value." No values, that is to
say opinions, exist in the absence of life. In the matter of such
a thing as an automatic switch we might consider that the
switch is capable of making a decision whether to be off or
on. However, we must remember that the original decision
that a switch was to be made, and that "off" and "on" could
be accomplished, and indeed, the design of a switch itself
depended entirely upon life quality.

In the field of mechanics we do not discover creativeness.
We discover varying conditions, varying arrangements, deter-
ioration and destruction of one or another form, but we do
not discover any alteration in quantity. Indeed, the entire
science of physics is predicated upon the assumption of "conservation of energy," which is to say that energy, itself, can-

not be created or destroyed but can only alter its form. To this we might add "conservation of space," "conservation of matter," and "conservation of time." None of these things are capable, in themselves, of altering. They are not capable of more than change of position or alteration of form. The physicist is very fond of demonstrating that the breaking of a vase does no more than the altering of the relative positions of the particles of the form, and that the burning of a piece of coal does not change the basic particles of matter, since if you were to collect all the smoke, and the ash, and the particles which radiated from the burning and weigh them you would have the same weight as before the coal was burned. In other words, the quantity of matter does not change, and, as above, it does not create to itself or add to itself in any way.

Life, it has been adequately established, can, however, create. It can create particles and it can add to mass. The demonstration of this on a man is an easily accomplished thing and is quite conclusive. A process known as "the remedy of havingness" is capable of altering the weight of a man upwards of twenty to thirty-five pounds even though there is no change whatsoever in the diet or the living habits of that person. In other words, the life which is in the body of the man, and which is actually the man, can, by a certain process, increase the amount of mass of this man. Another process known as "perfect duplication" can reverse this, and, again without change of diet or the living habits of the man, decrease the amount of mass of a man without the complications of heat or waste-products being present. Thus, forthrightly and directly, in the same frame of reference as that used by the physicist, it is easily demonstrated that life does create mass and can cause mass to disappear.

As long ago as fifty years, as represented by an article in the Encyclopaedia Britannica, it was fairly well understood that the study of physics should have begun with an examination of the mind. This article, under the heading of time and space, states that as space and time are mental phenomena their proper delineation and study begins in the field of the mind. Nineteenth century "mental sciences" were insufficiently schooled in science to comprehend this, and the physicist, unaware in general of such facts, did not consider that his proper province was the mind. Thus a misunderstanding existed in the Humanities and in the Sciences where one was depending upon the other, and the result came about that neither knew his proper field of endeavour. By undertaking a study of the mind from the orientation of physics, and with the application of all the principles known in chemistry, physics, and mathematics (items with which the nineteenth century psychologist was entirely unfamiliar, and which the twentieth century psychologist utterly disdains), it was only then possible to produce some comprehension of this thing we call life in this place we call the physical universe.

Thus, that thing which considers, that thing which has opinions, that thing which creates, that thing which monitors, that thing which has goals, desires, and which can experience, is Life. What we call space, time, energy, matter, forms of any kind, are the by-products of, and are monitored by, Life. Energy, whether in the form of a mental image, a body, a tree, or a rock, are alike the by-products of life. There is no faintest difference, save only density and wavelength, between the space you behold around you with your physical eyes and the spaces and forms you see when you close them and behold a mental image. These things, alike, are energies, and obey the various laws of energy.

Here, then, we have a unit or a quality capable of bringing into being quantities such as spaces, energies, masses, and time, capable of changing and controlling these masses and energies, capable of adding to them or subtracting from them.

There is considerable dissertation in "Dianetics: The Modern Science of Mental Health" concerning the "awareness of awareness unit." When this subject was first under investigation it was established that all was not a machine. Somewhere, in tracing back the various lines, it was necessary to strike a cause point, either simply to assume that there was a cause point or to discover one. Two words were used in connection with this causative agent. One of them was "analytical mind," and the other, much more properly, the "awareness of awareness unit." The awareness of awareness unit, as its name implies, is aware of being aware, or aware of being alive. When one was looking at or discussing the analytical mind, one was aware of something else: that the awareness of awareness unit became connected in some fashion with computers, or analyzers, in order to handle and control the remainder of the physical being. The term "analytical mind" then meant the awareness of awareness unit plus some evaluative circuit or circuits, or machinery, to make the handling of the body possible.

The other item discussed broadly in "Dianetics: the Modern Science of Mental Health," was the "reactive mind." This mind was a stimulus-response mind which depended for exterior direction upon its action and reaction. The reactive mind was conceived to be a collection of records, in picture form, so arranged as to make a complete pattern of experience, capable by its pattern alone of evaluating the conduct or behaviour of the individual. The pictures contained in the reactive minds are now called "facsimiles," for they are no more and no less than pictures, like photographs, taken of the universe around the individual and retained by him. A specialized kind of facsimile was the "engram." This differed from other mental pictures because it contained, as part of its content, unconsciousness and physical pain. The definition of an engram is: a picture of "a moment of pain and unconsciousness." The reactive mind was conceived to have more of these engrams than the analyzer. But the analyzer was seen to have some of these, too, except they were a lighter form and were a lock on the engram in the reactive memory bank. Indeed, when one considered the reactive mind he was actually considering what is, in the electronic brain, a memory bank. Instead of cards or a card-file system the reactive mind contained pictures. These pictures were filed and were drawn out of the files by the environment, which contained restimulators.* The presence of these pictures could alter form and could alter behaviour. The eradication of one of these engrams by one of the earlier erasure techniques of Dianetics was found to alter the stimulus-response behaviour of the individual.

Here we were confronting three kinds of mind. One was the causative agent, the awareness of awareness unit, which did not appear to have any by-products but which was impinged upon another mind called the analytical mind, which on a machine basis analyzed situations rationally, when sane and rational, and a third kind of mind even further remote from the awareness of awareness unit, which acted without the consent of the causative agent and did not in any way consult it. Now on a very careful review of this we see that the analytical mind and the reactive mind, alike, are by-product mechanical minds. Alike, they depend upon energy,

* See *restimulator* in Glossary starting on page 171.

spaces, storage, and other quantitative things. The awareness of awareness unit, however, is itself decision, is itself knowingness. It delivers into the analytical mind and its system various knowingnesses to be handled on a mechanical basis, and unwittingly delivers into the hands of the reactive mind—which is totally a mechanical thing—the right to alter and correct the analytical mind. Apparently, then, we have here a causative agent and two machines. We might as well, then, take the obvious conclusion that there is the awareness of awareness unit, and that this in some fashion handles machinery, and that the analytical mind, the reactive mind, and even the body and the environment are mechanical. One item here is qualitative and decisional—the awareness of awareness unit. All other items are subordinate to it and depend for their conclusions either upon it or upon the environment. Here again we have quality versus quantity.

A further demonstration of this awareness of awareness unit in action is quite convincing. A machine, a meter, which is built in every tradition of physics and electronics, and which is composed of nothing more or less than the usual meters and gauges and electrodes, can detect the production of energy by the analytical mind. This machine demonstrates conclusively that the awareness of awareness unit can predict and cause an energy reaction to occur at will. It goes further and demonstrates that the awareness of awareness unit can bring about, without further contact, an energy flow in a body at a distance. This is a very startling demonstration, and is one of the more significant electrical discoveries of recent times. The conditions of the experiment are sufficiently rigorous to dispel any doubt in the mind of a physicist concerning the authenticity of occurrence.

If there were no energy being created by the awareness of

awareness unit, then one would be at a loss to account for mental energy pictures, for these things, being made at a tremendously rapid rate, have considerable mass in them— mass which is measurable on a thing which is as common and everyday as a pair of bathroom scales.

As soon as it was discovered how facsimiles (these mental energy pictures) came into being it was also discovered that they were actual energy and not "an idea of energy" as they had been supposed to be in the past. The facsimile and the engram come into action by resistance. The awareness of awareness unit resists a scene in the physical universe, either resisting its approach or departure, and thus by this resistance makes a print. This print is made in a moving fashion, like a motion picture, and is complete in every detail. Later on the individual can call back this print and take a look at it, and will find it to have in it the exact forces which were in the original version in the physical universe. The awareness of awareness unit does this so easily that it has been completely unaware of what it was doing. Now, when the awareness of awareness unit makes a print, trying to restrain something from going away, or trying to restrain it from approaching, and considers that the survival of its body is being violated or threatened, it files this print in such a way that it will not have to look at it again. But this does not mean that an approximation of the print by the physical environment can-not reactivate the print independently. In other words, when the awareness of awareness unit puts away and does not want to look again at such a facsimile, the facsimile itself begins to have a power over the awareness of awareness unit. The collected files of these non-survival experiences come together and are the reactive mind. The awareness of awareness unit could be conscious of these, but chooses not to be. Thus the environment can restimulate this reactive mind and can cause changes of behaviour and bodily form such as over-weight, psychosomatic ills, or even fixed expressions or gestures.

The essence of time is change. Where there is no change there is no time. Thus, something which is unchanging is enduring. If a thing has no change in it, it will then "float" in all time, since it does not assign itself to any changingness, being a thing of no-change. Thus we discover that silences and no-motions "float" in time and we discover that every place on the time track where the awareness of awareness unit has taken a picture of silence, has resented or restrained silence, it then has an energy mass which will "float" or stay with it, whatever time it assigns to itself, and we get the composition of the physical universe. The physical universe is composed of "floating" or *forever* energy. If this did not work out in processing and if it were not a usable principle it would not be included in this text.

In view of the fact that these facsimiles, particularly those of silence, can "stay with" the individual, then we get the entire mechanism we call "restimulation" where the environment reactivates a facsimile, which then acts back against the body or awareness of awareness unit of the person. This is a very simple system of stimulus-response. We discover then that engrams, or facsimiles in general, have a tendency to hang up on all of their silent or motionless spots. Thus a facsimile may contain considerable action and yet be stuck at one point of no-motion. Here we have a no-motion on either side of which there is motion. The no-motion point hangs up and is not contacted by the awareness of awareness unit, since the awareness of awareness unit is looking, in general, for motion. Thus we get a phenomenon known as "stuck on the time track" where an individual can believe himself to be at some distant point in the past. The facsimile or engram in which he is "caught" has almost as much reality to him as a condition of existence as his present-time environment. When he becomes entirely psychotic the facsimile or engram has far more reality to him than his present-time environment. Thus we have aberration and psychosomatic illness.

In early Dianetics, the way this condition was alleviated was by addressing the pictures themselves and persuading the awareness of awareness unit to erase them by recounting them and re-experiencing them. Because this took a long time, and because auditors had a tendency to abandon half-erased incidents, the technology—while workable—was not conclusive. Thus, more research and investigation had to be entered upon in order to establish the best way to handle this situation.

CHAPTER III

THE AWARENESS OF AWARENESS UNIT

In examining the individuality and identity of the individual one discovers that the individual *is* himself, and not his by-products. The individual is not his analytical mind, he is not his reactive mind, he is not his body any more than he is his house or car. He might consider himself to be associated with his analytical mind, his reactive mind, his house, his body, his car, but he is not these things. He is himself. The individual, the personality, *is* the awareness of awareness unit, and the awareness of awareness unit is the person. As this awareness of awareness unit confuses itself further and further with the pictures it has made of its surroundings it conceives itself more and more to be an object, until at last when it has gone entirely down the tone scale* it has arrived at the point where its fondest belief is that it is an object.

Just as you would not say that John Jones was his car, so must you also say—when you perceive this clearly—that John Jones is not his analytical mind or his reactive mind, his body, or his clothes. John Jones is an awareness of awareness unit, and all there is of him that is capable of knowing and of being aware is John Jones, an awareness of awareness unit.

When we have arrived at a state where John Jones himself knows that he is an awareness of awareness unit and not his analytical mind, his reactive mind, his body, his clothes, his

* Tone-scale: gradation of levels of survival potential (see Glossary).

house, his car, his wife or his grandparents, we have what is called in Dianetics, a "Clear." A Clear is simply an awareness of awareness unit which knows it is an awareness of awareness unit, can create energy at will, and can handle and control, erase or re-create an analytical mind or reactive mind.

The difference of approach is this: instead of erasing all the things with which the awareness of awareness unit is in conflict, we make the awareness of awareness unit capable of besting and controlling all those things with which he thought he had to be in conflict. In other words, we raise the determinism of an individual up to a point where he is capable of controlling his mental pictures and the various by-products of life. When he is capable, so far as his ability is concerned, of controlling and determining the action of these things, he is no longer aberrated. He can recall anything he wants to recall without the aid and assistance of energy masses. He can be what he wants to be. He has had restored to himself a considerable freedom.

About the only difficulty we have in accomplishing this state of Clear, with all the power and ability appended thereto, is the fact that individuals come to believe that they have to have certain things in order to go on surviving. Actually, an awareness of awareness unit cannot do anything else but survive. He is unkillable, yet his by-products are destroyable, and confusing himself with his by-products he begins to believe that he has to have or do certain things in order to survive. His anxiety becomes so great on this that he will even believe that he has to have problems in order to survive. An awareness of awareness unit is very unhappy unless it has some mass or space of some kind and if it does not have various problems to solve.

For a very long time in Dianetics we looked far for the

"One-Shot Clear." Such a thing has come into existence and is workable on over fifty percent of the current populace of mankind. The One-Shot Clear depends, of course, upon getting the awareness of awareness unit at a distance from and in control of its various by-products so that it no longer confuses itself with its by-products. The astonishing speed with which fifty per cent of the human race can be cleared is believable only when you put it into action. The magic words are : "Be three feet back of your head." This is the One-Shot Clear. If the existence of a One-Shot Clear, or a process is indigestible to people it is because they have so long contemplated objects and have their attention so thoroughly fixed upon objects that they can no longer view space. And the idea of viewing space, the idea of being without objects is so antipathetic to them that they feel they must condemn any effort which might take from them the proximity of some of their fondest possessions.

It is so strongly antipathetic to Man to look at space that one of the basic processes of Dianetics—causing him to look at spots in space—will cause a rather low-toned individual to become quite violently ill at his stomach. The nausea resulting simply from contemplating empty space is discoverable only in those who have a great deal of trouble with possessions and who are unable to have things. From having to have things they have gotten to a point where they do not believe they can have anything any more. Thus, being asked to contemplate an emptiness of any kind is enough to cause a violent physical reaction. Hence, this whole subject of "Clear" and exteriorization, as it is technically termed, is very antipathetic to the remaining fifty percent of the human race who cannot be hit instantly with this one-shot button.

Fifty percent of the people you walk up to, if you do not

pre-select your preclears—a person on the road to being Clear—will immediately exteriorize, be a distance from their body, and behold themselves as capable of handling a great many things they before considered impossible to control the moment you say "Be three feet back of your head." The remaining fifty percent will look at you with varying puzzlement. These know they are a body. These know they are an object, and these know (most of them) that they would get sick at their stomachs if they contemplated being all by themselves in space. They would believe it would be impossible to control a body while being three feet behind it. Thus one gets into an immediate argument with such people, and they wish to go into the various deeper significances. If these people were lost to us with current Dianetic processes, we would still have gained many percentile over any past effort to do something for the race or about the mind.

In the past, even when we looked as short a time ago as 1949, we discovered that Man in general did not possess the ability to get a recovery percentage in patients higher than twenty-two percent. Oddly enough, whether it was a witch doctor at work, a psychoanalyst, psychologist, a medical doctor, or any other practitioner, simple assurance and a pat on the back yet brought about twenty-two percent cured. This fact, not looked at very carefully by practitioners, caused people to believe that the only thing that was wrong with the mind was that people thought something was wrong with the mind and all people needed was a cheering word and it would be all right. Twenty-two percent of a population will recover if anything is done for them. The remaining 78 percent are not quite so lucky. When we can raise the percentages even to 30 percent we are doing more than has ever been done before. When any practice gets less than 22 percent recovery, then that practice is actually definitely harming people, for if all the practitioner did was be at home in his office and give cheery reassurance to his patients he would get this 22 percent. He would have to be very active and depressive in order to decrease this amount of recoveries. Now, when we suddenly vault to the figure of 50 percent we know that we are closing with the answer. Thus, we could relax at this very point, confident that we have done more in this field than has ever before been done.

However, it is not good enough within our framework. In the first place, if we wish to help people involved with the government, people involved with ruling, people involved with the material sciences—such as physicists and chemists— we are dealing with almost entirely the remaining "resistive" 50 percent. This does not mean that a person, simply by exteriorizing, is weaker. It means that a person with continuous contact with the physical universe and continuous harassment and concern over the state of objects or energy is apt to get what we call "interiorized."

A recent series of cases undertaken to demonstrate how far we had to go and what we had to do in order to bring results in this remaining 50 percent has now concluded successfully. With modern techniques, very, very closely followed, auditors trained by the central organization have been successfully clearing cases which were resistive and did not improve on all earlier processes as of 1951, '52, '53 and the bulk of '54. The certainty of clearing the first 50 percent simply with the magic words has been followed now with a certainty of handling the remaining 50 percent. This presents a rather different scene and attitude than in 1950 when an auditor had to be "intuitive" and had to work endlessly, it seemed, to produce gains on cases, much less clearing. My own percentages in clearing people do not count, and I learned early (with some puzzlement) that what I did with a preclear and the results I obtained with a preclear were not the results which would be obtained by another auditor. It was this fact alone which caused research and investigation to be continued at such lengths, and processes to be codified so closely. For first we had to know processes, and then we had to know how to train auditors, and finally we are obtaining these clearing results.

Any Clear earlier obtained was known to be Clear simply by the fact that he could recall at will by pictures, or could perform certain other feats. Actually, a person was only able to stay Clear when he was not immediately involved with either his analytical or his reactive mind. And those Clears which remained stable had been put unwittingly into a much more advanced state than had been supposed, even by the auditor. It was an investigation of these Clears which led forward into the techniques we have now. It was found that many of them were simply wide-open cases which had become rather able to read their own facsimiles. Several had simply increased their ability to a point so senior to other people's ability that everyone agreed they should be called "Clear." And then there was the actual Clear. The actual Clear, on close questioning, even though he himself had not always noticed it, conceived himself now to be some distance from the body. Those Clears which remained stable and continued to perform and function despite the convulsions of life were these who had been stably exteriorized. This may be a datum which is very hard for some Dianeticists to assimilate, but again the difficulty would stem only from the fact that these would be unwilling to look at space or would be afraid of being disenfranchised. Such people are very frightened of losing their bodies. But this is a fact with which we cannot argue, that so far as psychosomatic illness is concerned it is best resolved by exteriorization. One has the individual step back from his body, look at it, and patch it up, and that is about all there is to psychosomatic illness. There is, of course, an electronic structure of the body which one can direct a person's attention to, but I have seen the shape of a face change in a moment, I have seen psychosomatic illnesses disappear in seconds, and as long as there was any physical structure left to work with at all I have seen the problem of psychosomatic illness pushed so far into the background, as a problem, that we no longer think in these terms and indeed do not consider Dianetics well used when it is only addressed to psychosomatic illness and aberrations.

Our emphasis today is upon ability. We have found that the more we increase the ability of a person the better the by-products around him become. Simply by increasing an individual's ability to walk or to talk we can change his physical beingness and his mental outlook.

By this theory it would be enough to have somebody learn how to make pottery, or drive a car, or sing or speak in public, to increase his mental and physical health. And indeed, on investigation we discover that these things are therapeutic, but we discover that they are limited in their therapy because the talents which an individual learns in this fashion are talents involved entirely with the handling and orientation of the body, and he is not being entirely influenced merely by his body. He is being influenced as well by the computing machinery which he calls his analytical mind and by the more insidious and less obvious machinery called his reactive mind. Furthermore, by these increases in ability he is not brought up to a point where he can control or handle his entire environment. Such an ability can be developed only by and in the awareness of awareness unit itself. When it is learning to do something via the body it is not learning to do something directly, it is learning to do something with help — the help of arms and legs, face, voice, eyes and thus hobby therapy is limited even though it is quite positive.

Looking a little further along this line one discovers that the awareness of awareness unit has peculiar abilities. First and foremost of its abilities is to be where it likes to be, and look. It does not need eyes. It does not need a vehicle in which to travel. All it needs to do is to postulate its existence in a certain location and then look from that point of existence. In order to do this it has to be willing to be cause. It has to be willing to be an effect. But if it can do this it can go much further—it can create and change space. Furthermore, it can erase at a glance facsimiles and engrams.

Now when we get into such capabilities people are liable to believe that we have entered the field of mysticism and spiritualism. But an inspection of these fields demonstrates the people in them not to be very able. Mysticism and other such practices are reverse practices. Rather than controlling the reactive bank, the analytical mind, the body, the environment, they seek very markedly to withdraw from the necessity to control. This is downward ability, and while I might be accused of maligning these fields, I can only look at the people I have known in these fields and at the fact that I, myself have studied in these fields in the East and know their limitations. People are apt to confuse exteriorization with astral walking. As you sit there reading this book you are definitely and positively aware of sitting there, and of this book. There is no question about whether or not you are looking at a book. You don't believe yourself to be projected, and you don't have to guess where you are, and you don't think you have to create some sort of an image in order to look at anything. You are simply sitting there reading a book. This is exteriorization. If you were cleared, and, with your body at home you were in a library, you could read in the library just as well, with the limitation that you might not have as good a grasp on pages. You would certainly know you were in the library. There would be no question about this. There would be no question about the text on the periodicals on the table. There would be no question about the quality and personality of the librarian and other people sitting there. Being Clear does not enter into guesswork. You would not be concerned with telepathy, with the reading of people's minds, and other such bric-a-brac. You would simply know what you wanted to know. Further, you wouldn't have to use a system for finding out what you know. You would simply know it.

If Man cannot face what he is, then Man cannot be free. For an awareness of awareness unit surrounded entirely by energy masses, and believing that it itself is completely these masses, is in a difficult and desperate state. It believes, for instance, that in order to go from one address to another it has to take the energy mass along with it. This is not true. One might carry a body around in order to speed up one's conversation, in order to have a problem, in order to get some attention and interest from people, but one would not carry a body around because one had to have a body.

The general attitude of a person who is cleared is the most interesting thing to observe. Only a cleared person has a very definite tolerance for the behaviour of others. People before they are cleared are in varying degrees of distrust of other people. They are hiding, or protecting, or owning things to such a degree that they do not dare separate themselves from them.

There is a certain fear of an exteriorized person. There is a belief that he might do them wrong. Actually one is done wrong by the weaklings of this world, not the strong men. One does not have to enslave and control by force those whose conduct he does not fear. When you find an individual who is bent entirely upon a course of the arduous control of the motions of others you are looking at an individual who is afraid. By their fear you shall know them.

Another slight difficulty in the state of exteriorization is that one has a tendency to let things be more or less as they are. Up to a certain point one is content to let the game run and take part in it and have fun with it. The point, of course, is the destruction of the playing field. Life, to a Clear, is no more and no less than a game, and the only thing which he would consider somewhat unpardonable in behaviour would be the wiping out of the playing field. But if he were even higher in such a state he should, theoretically, make his own playing field. However, if he did this he would find difficulty getting into communication with other live beings, unless, of course, he made them, which is rather an unsatisfactory state of affairs since one never quite forgets that he did so.

Moral conduct is conduct by a code of arbitrary laws. Ethical conduct is conduct out of one's own sense of justice and honesty. When you enforce a moral code upon people you depart considerably from anything like ethics. People obey a moral code because they are afraid. People are ethical only when they are strong. One could say that the criminals of earth are those upon whom moral codes have been too forcefully enforced. (As an example of this take the cliché object, the minister's son.) Ethical conduct does not mean promiscuous abandon or lawless conduct. It means conduct undertaken and followed because one has a sense of ethics, a sense of justice, and a sense of tolerance. This is self-determined morality. A Clear has this to a very marked degree. By actual check of many such cases their moral behavior is intensely superior to that of people who pride themselves on "being good." The point arises because law and order depends for its existence upon its necessity in the field of morals, and it looks with a sort of horror on somebody who would be good without recourse to or threat from the forces of law and order. Such a person would be rather hard to have around. He would cut down the number on the police force quite markedly.

The state of Clear, then, is attainable and is desirable, and now that we can accomplish it with greater positiveness than in 1950 is found to be superior to that described in the second chapter of "Dianetics : The Modern Science of Mental Health."

The way one goes about being Clear, or creating a Clear, is simple, but requires a certain code of conduct called The Auditor's Code, and requires, we have discovered, a considerable amount of training. Clearing another person is a highly specialized ability. This ability must be raised in individuals before they can easily and successfully undertake such a project. Witnessing this is the fact that while many of the processes involved in clearing have been available for a very, very long time, very few people have successfully used them. The discovery of why this was was quite as important as the state of Clear itself. The remedy of this disability lies in training and processing. The activity of creating a Clear is known as "processing" and is undertaken by one individual on behalf of another individual. "Self-clearing" has not been found possible where the individual was badly mired in his own case.

Enormously subordinate to the goal of Clear, but enormously senior to Man's various healing activities in the mind, spirit, and body, the very processes which lead up to Clear resolve, whether one wants them to or not, a great many of the physical and mental aberrations of the individual. One can take one of these processes and run it all by itself, and accomplish more with Dianetics than Man has previously accomplished in any of the fields that deal with human aberration. When one has the answer, of course applying those answers to minor psychosomatic difficulties, or aberrations, or spiritual unrest is elementary. But again we have discovered that there is no real substitute for training either at the hands of an already trained and skilled auditor, or best, from a central organization.

The awareness of awareness unit was not readily discoverable in the field of physics because physics is entirely concerned with mechanics. Physics starts with the assumption of the conservation of energy and the existence of space and goes on into further complexities from there. The awareness of awareness unit is one step earlier than all this, and its existence was unsuspected by a mis-definition in the field of physics. That was the definition of a static. A static, in physics, is called something which is "an equilibrium of forces." This object at rest in an equilibrium of forces is an interesting semantic puzzle. If we put a glass upon a table and then say that it is a static, we are telling a very bad lie. It is not in an equilibrium of forces. That glass happens to be travelling at 1,000 miles an hour just by reason of the fact that the earth is turning. It has seven other directions and speeds by reason of being part of the planet earth, the solar system, and this galaxy. It cannot, then, be considered at rest. Thus no object can be considered at rest unless one considers something relatively at rest. The glass is at rest in relationship to the table, but this is not the physical definition.

The definition of a static discloses something else of interest. There was a missing definition in the field of mathematics, and that was the definition of zero. The mathematician for ages has been using in all his formulas a wild variable without suspecting it was there. He did not really encounter it until he got into the higher fields of nuclear physics. At this time he encountered it so forcefully and knew it so little that he had to alter most of his mathematical conceptions in order to work with nuclear physics at all.

This wild variable was no less than zero. Zero, put down as a goose egg in many mathematical formulas, would introduce many interesting variables. In the first place an absolute zero has never been obtained in this universe. It has only been approached. That is in terms of temperature. That is in terms of non-existence. We can say there is zero of apples, but that is still a qualified zero. We can say there were no apples, but that is further qualified as being in the past. It is a past zero. We can say there will be no apples, and again we will have the zero qualified as being in the future. Zero was an absence of a thing, and this immediately violated the definition of zero being no thing. The absoluteness of *no thing* had to be examined while we were examining the field of the mind and actually led to some very astonishing discoveries with regard to Life itself and immediately pin-pointed the existence of the awareness of awareness unit.

The proper and correct definition of zero would be: "Something which had no mass, which had no wave length, which had no location in space, which had no position or relationship in time." This would be a zero. One could state it more shortly, if a little less correctly as: "something without mass, meaning, or mobility."

It would be almost impossible to detach a dyed-in-the-wool physicist from the concept that everything was a "something-ness" and that there was actually a "nothingness." However, there is a nothingness which has quality. It has potentials, it has ability. It has the ability to perceive, it has the ability to create, the ability to understand, and the ability to appear and disappear to its own satisfaction in various positions in space. Furthermore, this thing could, we have demonstrated conclusively, manufacture or cause to vanish space, energy and masses, and could, quite additionally, reposition time.

These new concepts are actually advances in the field of physics and mathematics, and from the viewpoint of the physicist and the mathematician would only incidentally apply to the mind.

From this data we get the basic definition of a static, which is: "An actuality of no mass, no wave-length, no position in space or relation in time, but with the quality of creating or destroying mass or energy, locating itself or creating space, and of re-relating time." And thus we have the definition of an awareness of awareness unit. It is the definition of a static. It does not have quantity, it has quality. It does not have mechanics, it can produce mechanics, and it does have ability.

The foremost ability of the awareness of awareness unit is to have an idea, and to continue that idea, and to perceive the idea in its continuance in the form of mass, energy, objects and time. In the field of Scientology the fact that this awareness of awareness unit can also control and even make physical bodies is almost incidental. That is only a specialized branch of the game. In Dianetics this is a very important function, for one in Dianetics is working with Man.

A static could also be called an orientation point. It would be from that point that it made and directed space, energy and objects. It would be from that point that it assigned meanings, and that we have an essential difference between the awareness of awareness unit and its by-products. These by-products we categorize as symbols. When we say "mechanics" we actually mean to some degree "symbols." A symbol is something that has mass, meaning, and mobility— three M's. That is the technical definition of a symbol. An orientation point is something that controls symbols. The difference in ability of an awareness of awareness unit is how much it is an orientation point in relationship to how much it believes itself to be a symbol, or to have mass, meaning and mobility. Reduction from the state of awareness is into the condition of the symbol—mass, meaning and mobility. To get a clear idea of this, you see the word "a" on this page. That has mass, even if very slight mass. It has meaning, since it conveys an idea when glanced at, and it certainly has mobility, since you can move the book around. Now you, looking at this book, have the role of an orientation point to the degree that you do not conceive yourself to have a fixed identity, a fixed position, a fixed mass. If you, looking at the book, have no real mass, if your name is not a tremendously fixed idea with you, and if you know you can move your body around without having to move with it, then you would very clearly and decisively be an orientation point. But if you think you have mass and are mass, and if you think you are your name, and if you think you have to move around only by moving the body around, then of course somebody else, something else, can be your orientation point. It may be your mother. It may be your home town, or, if you are a mystic, it might even be some spirit. You would think of yourself as a symbol. Similarly, a symbol does not remember anything more than it symbolizes, and thus your memory to a large degree might be the memory of past allies—people who took care of you and to whom you were attached affectionately—and if you were in a lecture you would probably take notes rather than remember what is being said. An orientation point has the power of memory without record. A symbol has the power of memory only to the degree that it is a record.

Thus we see that it is desirable that an individual does not identify himself with masses, but that he retain his ability to handle masses and objects and energies, to remember at will, without the need of records such as those in the reactive bank, or facsimile machines such as those in the analytical mind's bank.

In any good, thorough investigation, one investigates to see what he will discover and to find better ways to do things. In any reliable investigation report one tells what he discovered and reports its character and nature. In this science we are doing just that. When we talk of the awareness of awareness unit we are not talking to be pleasing, to win friends or influence professors, we are simply telling you what has been discovered after twenty-five years of research and investigation in the field of the mind having taken off from the platform of physics and mathematics rather than philosophy. The awareness of awareness unit is a fact. It is a demonstrable fact, and the best way to demonstrate it is to use the processes which accomplish it, and then discover that the individual

is more well, has a better memory, is better oriented, more
capable, is more ethical, happier, has better command of
time, can communicate better, is more willing to have friends,
is less anti-social than the average person, and has a greater
zest for living and getting things done. All these things can be
accomplished by test.

In 1950 we often had occasion to demonstrate the existence of the engram. It seemed to be highly in question
amongst those people who were extremely specialized—it said
on their diplomas—in the field of the mind. To be accomplished in the field of the mind and yet not know anything
about engrams or facsimiles would be an idiotic state indeed,
because the mind is composed of facsimiles and engrams, if
one wishes to examine it—or energy products. Well, then
(as now) we were only interested in results. What can we do
with this technology? If we can demonstrate with this technology that we can better the lives, tolerances, abilities of
those around us, then certainly we will have done something.
We have no place for philosophical argument concerning this
material. It is simply workable material. You do not argue
with the directions on how to open a vacuum packed can. If
you don't follow them you don't get the can open. Or, not
following them, and still being insistent upon it, you smash
the can and ruin the contents. One would not go into a
philosophic dissertation about the directions of opening a can.
Obviously they are written by somebody who knows how to
open cans, and any hours spent on getting this person to
demonstrate that he really could open cans would be wasted
time. The thing to do is simply read the directions, follow
them very closely, and see whether or not the can is opened.
Although this seems to be a very common sort of example to
apply to that noble creature, Man, it is nevertheless, the

bluntest statement that could be made about the status of Dianetics and Scientology and their uses and purposes.

Dianetics has as its goal the repairing and patching up of this thing called by the uninitiated, this civilization, taking its destiny out of the hands of madmen who think that the entire organism is simply a machine, and putting it in the hands of the same people, only this time with the ingredient of sanity added. There isn't even any point in trying to categorize Dianetics or say that it compares to psychology or mathematics or engineering, or any other activity, because it is obviously senior to all these activities and doesn't have to take any of these activities into account to work. All Dianetics needs to work is a trained auditor, a preclear, and a little time in which to accomplish its processes. If these ingredients—the auditor, the preclear, and a little time—were not available, then there would be no purpose in having any Dianetics at all, since there wouldn't be any human race.

The spirit in which these conclusions are advanced is intensely practical, and now that some nitwits who probably don't get along with their wives and hate dogs, but who have worked themselves into the position of being able to, can knock a couple of atoms together, either by orders or by actual skill, and so tear up a very nice playing field, the presence of Dianetics in this world is not simply a practicality, but an urgency.

CHAPTER IV

ACCENT ON ABILITY

Almost anyone realizes that he can be better than he is, that he can do things better than he has been doing them. It is an entirely different thing to ask someone to realize that he is ill, aberrated, or stupid. Why is it that a man can understand that he can be more capable and very often cannot understand that he is incapable? It would seem to follow that if a man realized that he could be more capable, then he would realize at once that he was, to some degree, less capable than he could be. For various reasons, however, this does not follow. One is confronted many times too often by his insistence upon brilliance of a very stupid man. It could be said with some truth that the person who asserts he needs to know no more to be fully as bright as his fellows, would, upon examination, be discovered to be quite deficient in capability and understanding.

Earth has had many examples of this. The Fascist is probably best described as a very stupid man who insists upon a *status quo* which is intolerable for all others, yet who believes himself to be brighter than all others. But even a Fascist of the most modern sort—the Fission Fascist—would be the first to admit that both he and others could do a better job of being fascistic.

The basic reason for this is a simple one, almost idiotically simple. One can understand understanding, and can see that understanding can increase. Stupidity, ignorance, illness, aberration, incapability are only a fall away from understanding and are, themselves, less understanding and so are less understandable. One does not understand that he might get worse, and so does not have any great communication with people who tell him that he will get worse. The dying man believes right up to the moment of his last breath, no matter what he is saying to his doctor and family, that he is going to get better. He has no understanding of that state of non-understandingness called death. One can understand the understandable. One cannot understand the incomprehensible because the definition of incomprehensibility is non-understandability. As I said, this is an almost idiotically simple situation.

Life in its highest state is understanding. Life in its lower states is in a lower level of understanding, and where life has ceased to function and has arrived at what one might call total incapability, there is no understanding at all.

In Dianetics and Scientology we have a great deal to do with this subject called understanding. Understanding has very specific component parts. These component parts are: Affinity, Reality, and Communication.

Affinity, Reality, and Communication form an interdependent triangle. It is easily discovered on some inspection that one cannot communicate in the absence of Reality and Affinity. Further, one cannot have a reality on something with which he cannot communicate and for which he feels no affinity. And similarly, one has no affinity for something on which he has no reality and with which he cannot communicate. Even more narrowly, one does not have affinity for those things on which he has no reality and on which he cannot communicate, and one has no reality on things which he has no affinity for and cannot communicate upon, and one cannot communicate upon things which have no reality to him and for which he has no affinity.

A graphic example of this would be anger. One becomes angry and what one says does not then communicate to the person at whom one might be angry. Even more crudely, the fastest way to go out of communication with a machine would be to cease to feel any affinity for it, and to refuse to have any reality upon it.

We call this triangle the ARC triangle. The precision definitions of these three items are as follows:

1. COMMUNICATION is the interchange of ideas or particles between two points. More precisely, the definition of Communication is: Cause, Distance, Effect with Intention and Attention and a duplication at Effect of what emanates from Cause.

2. REALITY is the degree of agreement reached by two ends of a communication line. In essence, it is the degree of duplication achieved between Cause and Effect. That which is real is real simply because it is agreed upon, and for no other reason.

3. AFFINITY is the relative distance and similarity of the two ends of a communication line. Affinity has in it a mass connotation. The word itself implies that the greatest affinity there could be would be the occupation of the same space, and this, by experiment, has become demonstrated. Where things do not occupy the same space their affinity is delineated by the relative distance and the degree of duplication.

These three items, Affinity, Reality and Communication, can be demonstrated to equate into Understanding. Above Understanding is Knowingness without formula or design, and this might be considered to be a unit activity. Dropping down from a complete Knowingness we would arrive into the realm of Understanding, for this is a Third Dynamic* manifestation peculiar to two or more individuals. Were you to be a clever mathematician, you could discover by Symbolic Logic how all mathematical formulas could be derived from this principle that Understanding is composed of Affinity, Reality, and Communication. No mathematics falling outside this triangle is valid mathematics to man. There is no additional factor in Understanding except Significance, but this, of course, is the idea or consideration mentioned in the Communication Formula (1., above).

It is a truism that if we could understand all Life we would then tolerate all Life. Further, and more germane to ability, if one could occupy the position of any part of Life, one would feel a sufficient affinity for Life to be able to merge with it or separate from it at will.

When we say "Life" all of us know more or less what we are talking about, but when we use this word "Life" practically, we must examine the purposes and behaviour, and in particular the formulas evolved by life in order to have the game called "Life."

When we say "Life" we mean Understanding, and when we say "Understanding" we mean Affinity, Reality, and Communication. To understand all would be to live at the highest level of potential action and ability. The quality of Life exists in the presence of Understanding—in the presence,

* See full list of Dynamics in Chapter XI.

then, of Affinity, Reality, and Communication. Life would exist to a far less active degree in the levels of misunderstanding, incomprehensibility, psychosomatic illness, and physical and mental incapabilities. Because Life is Understanding it attempts to understand. When it turns and faces the incomprehensible it feels balked and baffled. It feels there is a secret, and feels that the secret is a threat to existence.

A secret is antipathetic to Life, and therefore Life, in searching for those things which would seem to reduce it, will hit upon various secrets it must discover. The basic secret is that a secret is an absence of Life, and a total secret would be a total unlivingness.

Now let us look at this formula of Communication and discover that we must have a duplication at Effect of what emanates from Cause. The classic example here is a telegram sent from New York City to San Francisco which says "I love you." When it arrives in San Francisco the machinery of communication has perverted it so that it says "I loathe you." This failure of duplication is looked upon as an error, and would cause considerable problems and trouble. It could not be considered to be a very good communication. There was nothing wrong with the basic intention. There was nothing wrong with the Attention which would be given the wire in San Francisco. The only thing that was wrong was a failure to duplicate at Effect what emanated from Cause.

Now if Life is Understanding it would find it very hard to communicate with something which was non-understanding. In other words, Life, faced with a non-understanding thing, would feel itself balked, for Life, being Understanding, could not then become non-understanding without assuming the role of being incomprehensible. Thus it is that the seeker after secrets is trapped into being a secret himself.

Where one has an effect point which is an incomprehensible thing, and where one is occupying a cause point, in order to get any communication through to the effect point at all, it would be necessary for the one at cause point to somehow or another reduce his understandingness down towards incomprehensibility. The salesman knows this trick very well. He looks at his customer, recognizes his customer is interested in golf, and pretends to be interested in golf himself in order to have his customer listen to his sales-talk. The salesman establishes points of agreement and potential duplication, and then proceeds into a communication. Thus searchers after truth have often walked only into labyrinths of untruth—secrets—and have themselves become incomprehensible, with conclusions of incomprehensibility. Thus we have the state of beingness of the philosophical textbooks of Earth. A wonderful example of this is Immanuel Kant, the Great Chinaman of Königsburg, whose German participial phrases and adverbial clauses, and whose entire reversal of opinion between his first and second books balks all our understanding as it has the understanding of philosophic students since the late Eighteenth Century. But the very fact that it is incomprehensible has made it endure, for Life feels challenged by this thing which, pretending to be understanding, is yet an incomprehensibility. This is the grave into which so many philosophers walk. This is the coffin into which the mathematician, seeking by mathematics the secrets of the universe, eventually nails himself. But there is no reason why everyone should suffer simply because he looks at a few secrets. The test here is whether or not an individual possesses the power to Be at his *own determinism*. If one can determine himself to be incomprehensible at will, he can of course, then, determine himself to be comprehensible again. But if he is obsessively, and without understanding, being determined into incomprehensibility, then of course he is lost. Thus we discover that the only trap into which Life could fall is to do things without knowing it is doing them. Thus we get to a further delineation of the secret and we discover that the secret, or any secret, could exist only when Life determined to face it without knowing and without understanding that it had so determined this action. The very best great secret, then, would be something which made Life also tend to forget that it was looking at a secret.

One can always understand that his ability can increase, because in the direction of an increase in ability is further understanding. Ability is dependent entirely upon a greater and better understanding of that field or area in which one cares to be more able. When one attempts to understand inability he is of course looking at less comprehensibility, less understanding, and so does not then understand lessening ability anywhere near as well as he understands increasing ability. In the absence of understanding of ability we get a fear of loss of ability, which is simply the fear of an unknown, or a thought-to-be-unknowable thing, for there is less knowness and less understanding in less ability.

Because Life does not want to face things which are less like life, it has a tendency to resist and restrain itself from confronting the less comprehensible. It is the resistance alone which brings about the dwindling spiral, the descent into less ability. Life does not will this descent into less ability unless Life is cognizant of the principles involved. Life resists itself into this less-ability. There is a primary rule working here: that which one fears, one becomes. When one refuses to duplicate something, and yet remains in its environment, his very resistance to the thing he refuses to duplicate will cause him eventually to become possessed of so many energy pictures of that thing which he refuses to duplicate that he will, to have any mass at all, find himself in possession of those energy pictures, and without actually noticing when it happened, is very likely to accept, at their level, those things which he refused to duplicate earlier. Thus we get the riddle of the engram, the facsimile, if we understand, at the same time, that Life does not necessarily find it bad to have masses of energy around, and is, indeed, unhappy unless it does have some energy. For if there is no energy, then there is no game. Life has a motto: that any game is better than no game. And it has another motto: any havingness is better than no havingness. Thus we find individuals clutching to them the most complex and destructive of facsimiles imaginable. They do not necessarily want these complexities, and yet they want the energy or the game which these complexities would seem to offer them.

If you would make anyone well, you must then concentrate upon an increase of ability, an increase of understanding. The only reason bad things come to Life is because understanding has impressed further life into them. When an individual faces some secret, the fact that he is facing it and injecting life into it alone causes the secret to activate and have force in action. The only way a bad situation in existence can continue to have life is by taking life from nearby sources of communication. The bad things of life, then, have life only to that degree that understanding is invested in them. We have an example in poliomyelitis, which was at one time an extremely minor and unheard-of illness. By various publications, by a great deal of advertising, by many invitations to combat this illness, it is made to take prominence and manifest itself in this society. The only life, actually, which poliomyelitis has is the amount of life which can be invested in poliomyelitis. Yet, poliomyelitis, one thinks, would exist and continue its way if it were ignored. If one were to go on ignoring poliomyelitis, now that one knows about poliomyelitis, yes, this would be the case. It indeed would continue to exist even though everyone was studiously ignoring it. As a matter of fact it would get worse. If, however, it were to be completely understood, and if an ability on the part of individuals existed by which they could face it without having to resist it, then the matter would be solved.

One wonders why all the nurses and doctors in contagious wards do not immediately pick up the illness, and here we have another factor which is the same factor as understanding, but couched in a different way. People do not acquire obsessively those things which they do not fear. An individual has to resist something, has to be afraid of something, has to be afraid of the consequences of something before it could have any adverse obsessive effect upon him. At any time he could have a self-determined duplication of it, but this, not being obsessive, not being against his will, would not produce any ill symptom beyond the length of time he determined it.

Part of understanding and ability is control. Of course, it is not necessary to control everything everywhere if one totally understands them. However, in a lesser understanding of things, and of course in the spirit of having a game, control becomes a necessary factor. The anatomy of control is Start, Stop and Change, and this is fully as important to know as Understanding itself, and as the triangle which composes Understanding, Affinity, Reality, and Communication.

The doctors and nurses in a contagious ward have some degree of control over the illnesses which they see before them. It is only when they begin to recognize their inability to handle these ills or these patients that they, themselves, succumb to this. In view of the fact that of recent centuries we have been very successful in handling contagious diseases, doctors and nurses, then, can walk with impunity through contagious wards.

The fighters of disease, having some measure of control over the disease, are then no longer afraid of the disease, and so it cannot affect them. Of course, there would be a level of body understanding on this which might yet still mirror fear, but we would have the same statement obtaining. People who are able to control something do not need to be afraid of it, and do not suffer ill effects from it. People who cannot control things can receive bad effects from those things.

Here we have an example of what might happen in the realm of disease. How about human aberration? We discover that the sanitariums of the world are all too often inhabited, in addition to patients, by those persons who were formerly at work in these institutions. It is a rather shocking thing to discover in Ward Nine the nurse who was once supervisor of a mental hospital. Now here we have a condition where there was no control or understanding. People do not understand mental illness, aberration, insanity, neurosis. The first actual effort along this line which cut down the tally was Freudian Analysis, and yet this, requiring much too long, was not an effective weapon. These doctors and nurses in institutions who, then, are themselves patients in the same institutions knew definitely that they did not have any real control over insanity. Thus, having no control over it, they became subject to it. They could not start, stop and change insanity. The franticness of this state is represented by the mediaeval torture which has been utilized in such institutions as "cures." By "cured" the people in charge of such institutions merely meant "quieter." The natural course of existence would lead them to think in terms of euthanasia, and so they have—that it would be best to kill the patient rather than to have his insanity continue. And they have even accomplished this at the rate of two thousand mental patients a year dead under electric shock machines. And they have accomplished it by a very high percentage dead under brain operations. The only effectiveness of electric shock and brain operations would be to render the patient less alive and more dead, and the end-product achieved so many times of death, would of course be the only way to stop the insanity. These people, of course, could not envision the fact that immortality and insanity in a future generation would crop up as a problem. They had to conceive that if they killed the patient, or if they simply made him much quieter, they had then triumphed to some degree. In view of the fact that Man, sane or insane, is not to be destroyed according to law waives against this "solution."

With Dianetics, to use the study in a relatively narrow field of application, we have assumed some control over insanity, neurosis, aberrations, and can actually start, stop and change aberration. In the first book, "Dianetics: The Modern Science of Mental Health," techniques were present which would place in view, and then vanquish them, almost any mental manifestation known in the field of insanity and aberration. Where an auditor was unable to do anything for the insane or the neurotic, the fault (if fault there was) generally lay in the fact that the auditor was actually afraid. His fear was borne entirely out of his insecurity in starting, stopping and changing the condition.

In modern instruction at Academies of Scientology, there is little or no emphasis placed upon the case of the student, and yet when the student graduates he is discovered to be in a very high tone. The entire concentration is upon giving the student the ability to handle any and all types of case, and he

becomes sufficiently secure in his ability—if he is graduated—
to walk without any fear and considerable calm through any
and all areas of human aberration. He has been given the
technologies by which these misbehaviours of Life can be
controlled. In view of the fact that he can start, stop and
change them he need no longer fear them, and could with
impunity work around the insane if this were his mission.

The handling of psychosis, neurosis, and psychosomatic
illness do not happen to be the mission of the auditor.
Indeed, these things get well only if they are more or less
ignored. As long as the accent is upon ability any malfunc-
tion will eventually vanish. The mission of the auditor is in
the direction of ability. If he increases the general ability of
the preclear in any and all fields then, of course, any misabi-
lity such as those represented by psychosis, neurosis, and psychosomatic illness will vanish. The auditor, however, is not
even covertly interested in these manifestations. Around him
he sees a world which could be far more able. It is his
business to make it so. While business, in general, does not
recognize that there is anything wrong with its abilities, it can
recognize that its abilities can be better. One well-trained
auditor working with group processing in the United States
Air Force could treble the number of pilots successfully
graduated from a school, and could reduce the crash toll of
high-speed planes by fully three-quarters. This is not a wild
statement. It is simply an application of the research data
already to hand. The mission is greater ability, not an eradication of inability.

Just to give more understanding to those around him could
be said to be a sufficient mission for a well-trained auditor,
for by doing so he would certainly increase their ability. By
increasing that ability he would be able to increase their Life.

The common denominator of all neurosis, psychosis, aberration and psychosomatic ills is "can't work." Any nation which has a high incidence of these is reduced in production, and is reduced in longevity.

And what does he do about "how bad it is"? Well, if one depends upon others or the environment to do something about it, he will fail. From his viewpoint the only one who can put more Life, more Understanding, more Tolerance and more Capability into the environment is himself, just by existing in a state of higher Understanding. Without even being active in the field of auditing, just by being more capable, an individual could resolve for those around him many of their problems and difficulties.

The accent is on ability.

*Amongst the unable is the criminal, who is <u>unable</u> to think of the other fellow, <u>unable</u> to determine his own actions, is <u>unable</u> to, follow orders, <u>unable</u> to make things grow, is unable to determine the difference between good and evil is unable to think at all or the future — Anybody has some of these the criminal has <u>all</u> of them — *

CHAPTER V

THE AUDITOR'S CODE

There are several codes in Scientology and Dianetics. The only one that has to be obeyed if we wish to obtain results upon a preclear is The Auditor's Code, 1954. In the first book, "Dianetics: The Modern Science of Mental Health," we had an Auditor's Code which was derived more or less from an ideal rather than from practical experience. In the ensuing years a great deal of auditing has been done and a great many errors have been made by auditors. And when we have taken the common denominator of what has caused preclears to make small or negative progress, we discover that these can be codified so as to inform the auditor who wishes to get results what to avoid in his processing.

When a psychoanalyst or psychologist uses Dianetics he is very prone to be operating in his own frame of conduct. It is the conduct of the practitioner almost as much as the processes which makes Dianetics work. In psychoanalysis, for instance, we discover that the basic failure of Freud's work in practice and as used by analysts failed chiefly because of two things done by the analyst in a consultation room. Whatever the value of Freud's libido theory, the effectiveness was reduced by the analyst's evaluation for the patient. The patient is not allowed to work out his own problem, or to come to his own conclusions. He is given ready-made interpretations. In psychology there is no operating code, for clinical psychology is not much practised and is, indeed, outlawed in many states. While psychiatry might have a *modus operandi*, none of those conversant with this handling of the insane—the function of psychiatry—would call it a code intended to induce a better state of beingness in a patient.

In education, which is in itself a therapy, we discover an almost total absence of codified conduct beyond that laid down by school boards to regulate the social attitude of, and restrain possible cruelty in educators. Although education is very widespread, and indeed is the practice best accepted by this society for the betterment of individuals, it yet lacks any tightly agreed-upon method or conduct-codification for the relaying of data to the student. Custom has dictated a certain politeness on the part of the professor, or teacher. It is generally believed to be necessary to examine with rigour and thoroughness. Students are not supposed to whisper or chew gum, but education in general has no code designed to oil the flow of data from the rostrum to the student bench. On the contrary, a great many students would declare that any existing code was designed to stop any flow whatever.

Dianetics is in an interesting position in that it is itself, and although people may try to classify it with mental therapy, it is closer to the level of education so far as the society itself is concerned. Its goal is the improvement of the mind on a self-determined basis, and its intended use is upon individuals and groups. Because it is an accumulation of data which is apparently the agreed-upon factors from which existence is constructed, and although the simple perusal of this data very often frees an individual, it is also disseminated on an individual and group basis directly to individuals and groups, and is a form of self-recognition.

If you were to make the best progress along any highway

you would do well to follow the signs. In this Auditor's Code of 1954 we have a number of sign-posts, and if their directions are pursued a maximum of result will result. If they are not pursued, one is liable to find the preclear over in the ditch in need of a tow-truck in the form of a better auditor. Quite in addition to the command of the processes themselves, the difference between the Book Auditor and the Professional Auditor lies in the observance of this code. A very great deal of time is invested in the auditor at Academies of Scientology in demonstrating to him the effects of disobedience of this code and obedience of it, and in leading him to practise it closely. This supervision in the Academies is relatively simple. One takes a look at the class and finds somebody who is not in good shape. One discovers who audited him, and one then knows what auditor is not following the Auditor's Code. The offending student is then taken aside and briefed once more. A graduating auditor has to know this code by heart, and more importantly has to be able to practise it with the same unconscious ease as a pilot flies a plane.

THE AUDITOR'S CODE, 1954

1. Do not evaluate for the preclear.
2. Do not invalidate or correct the preclear's data.
3. Use the processes which improve the preclear's case.
4. Keep all appointments once made.
5. Do not process a preclear after 10.00 p.m.
6. Do not process a preclear who is improperly fed.
7. Do not permit a frequent change of auditors.
8. Do not sympathize with the preclear.
9. Never permit the preclear to end the session on his own independent decision.
10. Never walk off from a preclear during a session.
11. Never get angry with a preclear.

12. Always reduce every communication lag encountered by continued use of the same question or process.

13. Always continue a process as long as it produces change, and no longer.

14. Be willing to grant beingness to the preclear.

15. Never mix the process of Dianetics with those of various other practices.

16. Maintain two-way communication with the preclear.

This is actually The Auditor's Code, 1954, Amended, since it has one additional clause from the original release of this code—number 16 : "Maintain two-way communication with the preclear."

If one were to sort out these provisos he would discover that all of them were important, but that three of them were more vitally concerned with processing than the others, and that these three, if overlooked, would inevitably and always result in case failure. These three are the differences between a good auditor and a bad auditor. They are numbers 12, 13 and 16.*

In 12 we discover that the auditor should reduce every communication lag encountered by continued use of the same question or process. Almost every case failure contains some of this. The difference between a Professional Auditor and a Book Auditor is most visible in this and the other two provisos mentioned. A good auditor would understand what a

* This code (replaced in 1968) was extended to include:

17. Never use Scientology to obtain personal and unusual favours or unusual compliance from the preclear for the auditor's own personal profit.

18. Estimate the current case of your preclear with reality and do not process another imagined case.

19. Do not explain, justify or make excuses for any auditor mistakes whether real or imagined.

communication lag is—the length of time intervening between the asking of a question and the receiving of a direct answer to that question, regardless of what takes place in the interval—and he would be very careful to use only those processes on a preclear which the preclear could reasonably answer up to, and he would be quite certain not to walk off from a communication lag into which the session had entered. A bad auditor would believe, when he had struck a communication lag, that he had simply found a blind alley, and would hastily change to some other question.

In number 13 : "Always continue a process as long as it produces change, and no longer," we find the greatest frailty on the part of auditors. An auditor who is not in good condition or who is not well trained will "Q and A" with the preclear. When the preclear starts to change, the auditor will change the process. (By "Q and A" we mean that the answer to the question is the question, and we indicate a duplication.) Here we find an auditor possibly so much under the command of the preclear, rather than the reverse, that the auditor simply duplicates obsessively what the preclear is doing. The preclear starts to change, therefore the auditor changes. A process should be run as long as it produces change. If the preclear is changing that is what the auditor wants. If the auditor were to stop and change off to some other process just because the preclear had attained some change, we would discover some very sick preclears. Additionally, an auditor is liable to continue a process long after it has stopped producing change. He and the preclear get into a sort of a marathon, a machine-motivated grind, on Opening Procedure by Duplication, which probably after ten hours produced no further alteration in the preclear. Yet this pair might go to 50 hours with the process and would be quite disheartened to discover that for 40 hours nothing had happened. This, however, is much less harmful as an action than just changing a process simply because it is producing change.

The maintenance of two-way communication is the most touchy activity of auditing. An auditor being the auditor and concentrating upon control of the preclear, all too often forgets to listen when the preclear speaks. Many an auditor is so intent upon the process that when it produces a change which the preclear thinks he should advise upon, the auditor ignores him. Ignoring the preclear at a time when he wishes to impart some vital information generally sends the preclear directly into apathy. At the same time, an auditor should not permit the preclear to keep on talking forever, as in the case of a lady recently reported who talked to the auditor for three days and three nights. The therapeutic value of this was zero, for the auditor was listening to a machine, not to a preclear. One should understand rather thoroughly the difference between an obsessive, or compulsive communication line and an actual communication. Listening to circuits* of course validates circuits. The auditor should pay attention to the rational, the usual, the agreed-upon, and should leave very much alone the bizarre, the freaky, the compulsive and the obsessive manifestations of the preclear. The maintenance of two-way communication is actually a process in itself, and is the first and most basic process of Dianetics, and continues on through all the remaining processes.

Simply because we have pin-pointed three of these there is no reason to ignore the others. Every time there has been a "psychotic break" by reason of or during auditing, it has occurred when the processing was being done late at night, when the preclear was improperly fed, when the preclear

* Circuits: Reactive patterns rather than actual communication. See Glossary.

had had a frequent change of auditors, and when two-way communication had not been maintained and the effort on the part of the preclear to impart a vital change to the auditor was ignored. All these "psychotic breaks" were repaired, but because these factors were present the patching up was rather difficult. Audit them early, audit them bright, listen to what they have to say about what's happening, make sure they are eating regularly, and change auditors on a preclear as seldom as possible, and no "psychotic breaks" will occur.

If you are simply investigating Dianetics to discover whether or not it is workable, you should be aware of the fact that the Auditor's Code, following of, is an essential portion of Dianetics. Dianetics functions very poorly in the absence of the Auditor's Code. It is part of the process, not simply a polite way to go about handling people. Thus, if Dianetics is tested in the absence of The Auditor's Code, do not pretend that it has been tested at all.

Another phrase might have been added to this code, but it would be more germane to living than to auditing, and that phrase would be: "Maintain silence around unconscious or semi-conscious people." The reason for this is contained in "Dianetics: The Modern Science of Mental Health" and in preventive Dianetics. Such statements become "engramic." The addition of this to the Auditor's Code, however, is not practical, as an auditor often finds himself talking to a "groggy" preclear. Because the auditor is reducing every communication lag he encounters by a repetition of the question, the asking of a question or giving of a command to a semi-conscious preclear is thus rendered relatively unaberrative, for sooner or later the question imbedded in the unconsciousness will work loose and the communication lag will not flatten until this occurs. Thus, simply the reduction of the communication lag in itself eradicates such phrases. Thus, this is not part of the Auditor's Code. However, when we encounter unconsciousness or semi-consciousness, as in moments immediately after the injury of a child, a street accident, an operation, we maintain silence for we are not auditing the person. Mothers and fathers would spare themselves a great deal of later mental unrest on a child's part if they knew and would follow this injunction, and in many other ways it is a very important one. A man can be killed by too much conversation around him while he is injured. No matter how deeply unconscious he may appear to be, something is always registering. The questioning by the police at the scene of an accident, where the person being questioned is in a state of shock, or where other accident victims are present, is probably the most aberrative conduct in this society. The questioning by police is quite restimulative in any event, and many severe complications after accidents have been traced immediately to this activity on the part of the police. It might be very important for some ledger somewhere to know exactly who caused this. It is more important that the people involved in it live and be happy afterward. It is not that we do not like police. This is not the case. We simply believe that the police should be civilized, too.

Simply memorizing this code is not enough. Memorizing it in order to practise it is indicated, but it is the practice of this code which is important. Observance of it is the hallmark of a good auditor, and it signalizes the recovery of the case.

If an auditor is going to raise the ability of the preclear, his ability in the field of auditing must be considerable. That ability begins with the understanding and observance of the Auditor's Code, 1954, Amended.

CHAPTER VI

TRAPPED

In Greece, Rome, England, Colonial America, France and Washington, a great deal of conversation is made on the subject of Freedom. Freedom, apparently, is something that is very desirable. Indeed, Freedom is seen to be the goal of a nation or a people. Similarly, if we are restoring ability to the preclear we must restore Freedom. If we do not restore Freedom we cannot restore ability. The muscle-bound wrestler, the tense driver, the rocket jockey with a frozen reaction time alike are not able. Their ability lies in an increase of Freedom, a release of tension, and a better communication to their environment.

The main trouble with Freedom is that it does not have an anatomy. Something that is free is free. It is not free with wires, vias, by-passes, or dams, it is simply free. There is something else about Freedom which is intensely interesting, it cannot be erased. In "Dianetics: The Modern Science of Mental Health" we learned that pleasure moments were not erasable. The only thing that was erasable was pain, discomfort, distortion, tenseness, agony, unconsciousness. In more modern Scientological parlance, Freedom cannot be "as-ised," it is something which is imperishable. You may be able to concentrate somebody's attention on something that is not free and thus bring him into a state of belief that Freedom does not exist, but this does not mean that you have erased the individual's freedom. You have not. All the freedom he ever had is still there. Furthermore Freedom has no quantity, and by definition it has no location in space or time. Thus we see the awareness of awareness unit as potentially the freest thing there could be. Thus man concentrates on Freedom.

But if Freedom has no anatomy, then please explain how one is going to attain to something which cannot be fully explained. If anyone talks about a "road to Freedom" he is talking about a linear line. This, then, must have boundaries. If there are boundaries there is no freedom. This brings the interesting proposition to mind that the very best process, by theory, would be to have an individual assume himself to be free, and then he would simply be asked to assume himself to be free again. Indeed, upon many cases of a high toned variety this is a quite workable process. An individual is "sick," he is usually in very good tone, the auditor simply asks him to assume that he is free, and he will cease to be "sick." The magic, however, is limited to those people who have some concept of what "free" means. Talk to a person who works from eight o'clock until five with no goals, and no future, and no belief in the organization and its goals, who is being required by time-payments, rent, and other barriers of an economic variety to invest all of his salary as soon as it is paid, and we have an individual who has lost the notion of Freedom. His concentration is so thoroughly fixed upon barriers that Freedom has to be in terms of less barriers. Thus, in processing we have to audit in the direction of less and less barriers in order to attain Freedom.

If Freedom is so very compelling and is so useful, and is in itself something like a synonym for ability—even if not entirely—then it is our task to understand a little more about Freedom as itself in order to accomplish its attainment, for unfortunately it is not enough for the bulk of the human race simply to say "be free" and have an individual recover.

Life is prone to a stupidity in many cases in which it is not cognizant of a disaster until the disaster has occurred. The middle-western farmer had a phrase for it: "Lock the door after the horse is stolen." It takes a disaster in order to educate people into the existence of such a disaster. This is education by pain, by impact, by punishment. Therefore, a population which is faced with a one-shot disaster which will obliterate the sphere would not have a chance to learn very much about the sphere before it was obliterated. Thus, if they insisted upon learning by experience in order to prevent such a disaster, they would never have the opportunity. If no atomic bomb of any kind had been dropped in World War II it is probable there would be no slightest concern about atomic fission, although atomic fission might have developed right on up to the planet-buster without ever being used against Man, and then the planet-buster being used on Earth and so destroying it.

If a person did not know what a tiger was, and we desired to demonstrate to him that no tigers were present, we would have a difficult time of it. Here we have a freedom from tigers without knowing anything about tigers. Before he could understand an absence of tigers he would have to understand the presence of tigers. This is the process of learning we know as "by experience."

In order to know anything, if we are going to use educational methods, it is necessary then to know, as well, its opposite. The opposite of tigers probably exists in Malayan jungles where tigers are so frequent that the absence of tigers would be a novelty, indeed. A country which was totally burdened by tigers might not understand at all the idea that there were no tigers. In some parts of the world a great deal of argument would have been entered into with the populace of a tiger-burdened area to get them to get any inkling of what an absence of tigers would be. Many cases in processing have suddenly lost a somatic,* to discover themselves in a new and novel state. This somatic was so routine and so constant and so pervasive that they could not intellectually conceive of what life would be like without that particular somatic.

The understanding of Freedom, then, is slightly complex in that individuals who do not have it are not likely to understand it, and thus we find an individual who knows nothing about exteriorization and knows everything about being in constant contact with the sensations of a body failing to grasp the idea of the freedom resulting from exteriorization. These people do not even believe that exteriorization can exist, and so combat it. They are so little experienced on the subject of Freedom that this type of Freedom is "known to be non-existent" to them.

The way to demonstrate the existence of Freedom is to invite the individual to experience Freedom, but if he does not know what Freedom is, then he will not exteriorize. We have to hit some sort of gradient scale on the matter, or make him turn around and look squarely at the opposite of Freedom.

But the opposite of Freedom is slavery and everybody knows this—or is it? I do not think these two things are a dichotomy. Freedom is not the plus of a condition where slavery is the minus unless we are dealing entirely with the political organism. Where we are dealing with the individual

* Somatic: A physical condition or sensation. See Glossary.

better terminology is necessary and more understanding of the anatomy of minus-Freedom is required.

Minus-Freedom is entrapment. Freedom is the absence of barriers. Less Freedom is the presence of barriers. Entirely minus-Freedom would be the omnipresence of barriers. A barrier is matter or energy or time or space. The more matter, energy, time or space assumes command over the individual the less Freedom that individual has. This is best understood as entrapment since slavery connotates an intention, and entrapment might be considered almost without intention. A person who falls in a bear-pit might not have intended to fall into it at all, and a bear-pit might not have intended a person to fall upon its stake. Nevertheless, an entrapment has occurred. The person is in the bear-pit.

If one wants to understand existence and his unhappiness with it, he must understand entrapment and its mechanisms.

In what can a person become entrapped? Basically and foremost, he can become entrapped in ideas. In view of the fact that freedom and ability can be seen to be somewhat synonymous, then ideas of disability are first and foremost an entrapment. I dare say that amongst men the incident has occurred that a person has been sitting upon a bare plain in the total belief that he is entirely entrapped by a fence. There is that incident mentioned in "Self-Analysis" of fishing in Lake Tanganyika where the sun's rays, being equatorial, pierce burningly to the lake's bottom. The natives there fish by tying a number of slats of wood on a long piece of line. They take either end of this line and put it in canoes, and then paddle the two canoes to shore, the slatted line stretching between. The sun shining downward presses the shadows of these bars down to the bottom of the lake and thus a cage of shadows moves inward towards the shallows. The fish, seeing this cage contract upon them, which is composed of nothing but the absence of light, flounder frantically into the shallows where they cannot swim and are thus caught, picked up in baskets and cooked. There is nothing to be afraid of but shadows.

When we move out of mechanics man finds himself on unsure ground. The idea that ideas could be so strong and pervasive is foreign to most men. For instance, a government attacked by the Communists does not perceive that it is being attacked only by ideas. It believes itself to be attacked by guns, bombs, armies and yet it sees no guns, bombs, armies. It sees only men standing together exchanging ideas. Whether or not these ideas are sound or not is beside the point, they are at least penetrative. No 16-inch armour plate could possibly stop an idea. Thus a country can be entrapped, taken and turned towards Communism simply by the spread of the Communistic idea. A country that fails to understand this arms itself, keeps its guns cocked, its armies alert, and then succumbs at last to the idea now entered into the heads of the armed forces, which it so hopefully employed. The collapse of Germany in World War I was an instance of this. Its armies, its grand fleet were all flying the red flag. Although Allied pressure and the conditions of starvation in Germany had much to do with its defeat, nevertheless, it was keyed into being by the Communist idea infiltrated into the minds of the men who originally were armed and trained to protect Germany. And Communism, just as an idea, traps the minds of men. They find themselves organized into cells, they find their customs abandoned and are regimented by a militant biological, soulless tyranny, their master. Here is an idea becoming a sort of trap.

So, first and foremost, we have the idea. Then, themselves

the product of ideas, we have the more obvious mechanics of entrapment in matter, energy, space and time.

The most common barrier which man recognizes as such would be a wall. This is so obviously a barrier that individuals quite commonly suppose all barriers to be composed of solid walls. However, almost any object can be made into a barrier. A less common use of an object as a barrier would be one which inhibited, by some sort of suction or drag, a departure from it. A solid lump of considerable magnetic properties will hold to it a piece of steel. Gravity is, then, a barrier of a kind. It holds the people or life units of Earth to Earth.

Another barrier would be energy. A sheet of energy or something carrying energy, such as an electrical fence, can prove to be a formidable barrier. A cloud of radioactive particles obstructing passage into another space could also be a barrier. Tractor-type beams, as in the case of gravity, could be seen to be a barrier of sorts, but in the form of energy.

Yet another barrier, easily understood, is that of space. Too much space will always make a barrier. Space debars an individual from progressing into another part of the galaxy. One of the finest prisons one could imagine would be one located on a small piece of matter surrounded by such a quantity of space that no-one could cross it. Space is such an efficient barrier that people in the Southwest of the United States, committing crimes, discover their way everywhere blocked by the giganticness of space. In New York City it would be very easy for them, after the commission of a crime, to vanish, but in attempting to cross a space of such size as the Southwest they become exposed everywhere to view, there being nothing else upon which the police can fix their attention.

Quite another barrier, less well understood, but extremely thorough as a barrier, is time. Time debars your passage into the year 1776 and prevents your repossession of things which you had in your youth. It also prevents you from having things in the future. Time is an exceedingly effective barrier. The absence of time can also be a barrier, for here an individual is unable to execute his desires and is so constricted by the pressure of time itself.

Matter, energy, space and time can all, then, be barriers. An awareness of awareness unit, however, which is the personality and beingness unit of the person, and which is composed of quality, not quantity, can be anywhere it wishes to be. There is no wall thick enough, nor any space wide enough, to debar the reappearance at some other point of an awareness of awareness unit. In that this *is* the individual, and not some ghost of the individual, and as the individual is himself an awareness of awareness unit and not his machinery and his body, we see that as soon as one understands completely that he is an awareness of awareness unit, he no longer is restricted by barriers. And thus those who would seek entrapment for individuals are entirely antipathetic towards the idea of exteriorization, and the person who knows nothing but barriers is apt to believe that a condition of no-barriers could not exist. Yet a condition of no-barriers can exist, and this is itself Freedom.

Examining Freedom, then, we have to examine why people do not attain it easily or understand it. They do not attain Freedom because their attention is fixed upon barriers. They look at the wall, not the space on either side of the wall. They have entities and demon-circuits* which demand their attention, and, indeed, the body itself could be con-

* Demon-circuits: Reactive mechanisms. See Glossary.

sidered to be an attention-demanding organism. One might believe that its total function was to command interest and attention. It is so interesting that people do not conceive that behind them lies all the Freedom anybody ever desired. They even go so far as to believe that freedom is not desirable and that if they could attain it they would not want it. One is reminded of prisoners who occasionally go so sufficiently "stir-crazy" as to demand after their release from prison confining walls and restricted spaces. Manuel Komroff once wrote a very appealing story on this subject, the story of an old man who had served twenty-five years in prison, or some such time, and who on his release asked for nothing more than the smallest room in his son's house and was happiest when he could see someone on an opposite roof who had the appearance of a guard, and who actively put bars back on his window. One could consider that a person who has been for a long time in the body could have such a fixation upon the barriers imposed by the body, that once an auditor tries to remove them the preclear puts them back quickly. You might say that such a person is "stir-crazy," yet the condition is remediable.

The anatomy of entrapment is an interesting one, and the reason why people get entrapped, and, indeed, the total mechanics of entrapment are now understood. In Scientology a great deal of experimentation was undertaken to determine the factors which resulted in entrapment, and it was discovered that the answer to the entire problem was two-way communication.

Roughly, the laws back of this are: Fixation occurs only in the presence of one-way communication. Entrapment occurs only when one has not given or received answers to the things

entrapping him. Thus we see the ARC Triangle itself, and
most importantly the Communication factor of that triangle,
looming up to give us Freedom.

It could be said that all the entrapment there is is the
waiting one does for an answer.

Here we find Man. Basically he is an awareness of awareness unit which is capable of, and active in, the production
of matter, energy, space and time as well as ideas. We discover that he is more and more fixated upon ideas, matter,
energy, space and time and the processes and functions
involving these. And we discover that these, being the products of the awareness of awareness unit, do not supply answers to the awareness of awareness unit unless the awareness of awareness unit supplies itself those answers.

Entrapment is the opposite of Freedom. A person who is
not free is trapped. He may be trapped by an idea, he may
be trapped by matter, he may be trapped by energy, he may
be trapped by space, he may be trapped by time, he may be
trapped by all of them. The more thoroughly a preclear is
trapped the less free he is. He cannot change, he cannot
move, he cannot communicate, he cannot feel affinity and
reality. Death itself could be said to be Man's ultimate in
entrapment, for when a man is totally entrapped he is dead.

It is our task in investigation and auditing to discover for
the individual and the group a greater freedom, which is the
roadway to a greater ability.

The processes the auditor uses today are designed entirely
to secure greater freedom for the individual, for the group,
for Mankind. Any process which leads to a greater freedom

for all Dynamics is a good process. It should be remembered, however, that an individual functions on all Dynamics, and that suppression by an individual of the Third or Fourth Dynamic leads to less Freedom for the individual, himself. Thus, the criminal, in becoming immorally free, harms the group and harms Mankind, and thus becomes less free himself. Thus there is no Freedom in the absence of Affinity, Agreement, and Communication. Where an individual falls away from these his freedom is sharply curtailed and he finds himself confronted with barriers of magnitude.

The component parts of Freedom, as we first gaze upon it, are then : Affinity, Reality, and Communication, which summate into Understanding. Once Understanding is attained, Freedom is obtained. For the individual who is thoroughly snarled in the mechanics of entrapment, it is necessary to restore to him sufficient communication to permit his ascendence into a higher state of understanding. Once this has been accomplished his entrapment is ended.

None of this is actually a very difficult problem. In the auditing done today it is very simple. But where the auditing is being done by a person who does not basically desire the freedom of the individual a further entrapment is more likely to ensue than further freedom. The obsessively entrapped are then enemies of the preclear, for they will trap others.

A greater freedom can be attained by the individual. The individual does desire a greater freedom, once he has some inkling of it. And auditing according to the precision rules and codes of Dianetics and Scientology steers the individual out of the first areas of entrapment to a point where he can gain higher levels of Freedom, either by further auditing or by himself. The only reason we need a regimen with which to begin is to start an individual out of a mirror-maze of such complexity that he himself, in attempting to wend his way, only gets lost.

This is Dianetics 55 !

CHAPTER VII

COMMUNICATION

Communication is so thoroughly important today in Dianetics and Scientology, as it always has been on the whole track, that it could be said that if you would get a preclear into communication you would get him well. This factor is not new in psychotherapy, but concentration upon it is new, and interpretation of ability as communication is entirely new.

If you were to be in thorough and complete communication with a car on a road, you would certainly have no difficulty driving that car. But if you were in only partial communication with the car and in no communication with the road, it is fairly certain that an accident would occur. Most accidents do occur when the driver is distracted by an argument he has had, or by an arrest, or by a cross alongside of the road that says where some motorists got killed, or by his own fears of accidents.

When we say that somebody should be in present time we mean he should be in communication with his environment. We mean, further, that he should be in communication with his environment as it exists, not as it existed. And when we speak of prediction we mean that he should be in communication with his environment as it will exist, as well as it exists.

If communication is so important, what is communication? It is best expressed as its formula, which has been isolated, and by use of which a great many interesting results can be brought about in ability changes.

There are two kinds of communication, both depending upon the viewpoint assumed. There is outflowing communication and inflowing communication. A person who is talking to somebody else is communicating to that person (we trust), and the person being talked to is receiving communication from that person. Now, as the conversation changes, we find that the person who has been talked to is now doing the talking, and is talking to the first person, who is now receiving communication from him.

A conversation is the process of alternating outflowing and inflowing communication, and right here exists the oddity which makes aberration and entrapment. There is a basic rule here: He who would outflow must inflow—he who would inflow must outflow. When we find this rule overbalanced in either direction we discover difficulty. A person who is only outflowing communication is actually not communicating at all in the fullest sense of the word, for in order to communicate entirely he would have to inflow as well as outflow. A person who is inflowing communication entirely is again out of order, for if he would inflow he must then outflow. Any and all objections anyone has to social and human relationships is to be found basically in this rule of communication, where it is disobeyed. Anyone who is talking, if he is not in a compulsive or obsessive state of beingness, is dismayed when he does not get answers. Similarly, anyone who is being talked to is dismayed when he is not given an opportunity to give his reply.

Even hypnotism can be understood by this rule of communication. Hypnotism is a continuing inflow without an opportunity on the part of the subject to outflow. This is carried on to such a degree in hypnotism that the individual is actually trapped in the spot where he is being hypnotized, and will remain trapped in that spot to some degree from there on. Thus, one might go so far as to say that a bullet's arrival is a heavy sort of hypnotism. The individual receiving a bullet does not outflow a bullet, and thus he is injured. If he could outflow a bullet immediately after receiving a bullet, we could introduce the interesting question, "Would he be wounded?" According to our rules he would not be. Indeed, if he were in perfect communication with his environment he could not even receive a bullet injuriously, but let us look at this from a highly practical viewpoint.

As we look at two life units in communication we can label one of them "a" and the other one of them "b." In a good state of communication "a" would outflow and "b" would receive, then "b" would outflow and "a" would receive. Then "a" would outflow and "b" would receive. In each case both "a" and "b" would know that the communication was being received and would know what and where was the source of the communication.

All right, we have "a" and "b" facing each other in a communication. "A" outflows. His message goes across a distance to "b" who inflows. In this phase of the communication "a" is Cause, "b" is Effect, and the intervening space we term the Distance. It is noteworthy that "a" and "b" are both life units. A true communication is between two life units, it is not between two objects, or from one object to one life unit: "a," a life unit, is Cause, the intervening space is Distance, "b," a life unit, is Effect. Now a completion of this communication changes the roles. Replied to, "a" is now the Effect, and "b" is the Cause. Thus we have a cycle which completes a true communication. The cycle is Cause, Distance, Effect, with Effect then becoming Cause and communicating across a Distance to the original source, which is now Effect, and this we call a two-way communication.

As we examine this further we find out that there are other factors involved. There is "a's" intention. This, at "b" becomes attention, and for a true communication to take place, a duplication at "b" must take place of what emanated from "a." "A" of course, to emanate a communication, must have given attention to "b," and "b" must have given to this communication some intention, at least to listen or receive, so we have both Cause and Effect having intention and attention.

Now there is another factor which is very important. This is the factor of duplication. We could express this as Reality, or we could express it as Agreement. The degree of Agreement reached between "a" and "b" in this communication cycle becomes their Reality, and this is accomplished mechanically by Duplication. In other words, the degree of Reality reached in this communication cycle depends upon the amount of duplication. "B," as Effect, must to some degree duplicate what emanated from "a," as Cause, in order for the first part of the cycle to take effect, and then "a," now as Effect, must duplicate what emanated from "b" for the communication to be concluded. If this is done there is no aberrative consequence. If this duplication does not take place at "b" and then at "a" we get what amounts to an unfinished cycle of action. If, for instance, "b" did not vaguely duplicate what emanated from "a" the first part of the cycle of communication was not achieved, and a great deal of randomity, argument, explanation, might result. Then if "a" did not duplicate what emanated from "b" when "b" was cause on the second cycle, again an uncompleted cycle of communication occurred with consequent unreality. Now naturally, if we cut down Reality, we will cut down Affinity, so where duplication is absent Affinity is seen to drop. A complete cycle of communication will result in high Affinity and will, in effect, erase itself. If we disarrange any of these factors we get an incomplete cycle on communication and we have either "a" or "b" or both *waiting* for the end of cycle. In such a wise the communication becomes aberrative.

The word "aberrate" means to make something diverge from a straight line. The word comes basically from optics. Aberration is simply something which does not contain straight lines. A confusion is a bundle of crooked lines. A mass is no more and no less than a confusion of mis-managed communication. The energy masses and deposits, the facsimiles and engrams surrounding the preclear are no more and no less than unfinished cycles of communication which yet wait for their proper answer at "a" and "b."

An unfinished cycle of communication generates what might be called "answer hunger." An individual who is waiting for a signal that his communication has been received is prone to accept any inflow. When an individual has, for a very long period of time, consistently waited for answers which did not arrive, any sort of answer from anywhere will be pulled in to him, by him, as an effort to remedy his scarcity of answers. Thus he will throw engramic phrases in the bank into action and operation against himself.

Uncompleted cycles of communication bring about a scarcity of answers. It does not much matter what the answers were or would be as long as they vaguely approximate the subject at hand. It does matter when some entirely unlooked for answer is given, as in compulsive or obsessive communication, or when no answer is given at all.

Communication itself is aberrative only when the emanating communication at Cause was sudden and *nonsequitur* to the environment. Here we have violation of attention and intention.

The factor of interest also enters here but is far less important, at least from the standpoint of the auditor. Nevertheless it explains a great deal about human behaviour, and explains considerable about circuits. "A" has the intention of interesting "b." "B," to be talked to, becomes interes*ting*. Similarly "b," when he emanates a communication, is interes*ted* and "a" is interes*ting*. Here we have, as part of the communication formula (but as I said, a less important part) a continuous shift from being interested to being interesting on the part of either of the terminals, "a" or "b." Cause is interes*ted*, Effect is interes*ting*.

Of some greater importance is the fact that the intention to be received, on the part of "a" places upon "a" the necessity of being duplicatable. If "a" cannot be duplicatable in any degree, then, of course, his communication will not be received at "b," for "b," unable to duplicate "a," cannot receive the communication. As an example of this, "a," let us say, speaks in Chinese, where "b" can understand only French. It is necessary for "a" to make himself duplicatable by speaking French to "b" who only understands French. In a case where "a" speaks one language, and "b" another, and they have no language in common, we have the factor of mimicry possible and a communication can yet take place.

"A," supposing he has a hand, could raise his hand. "B," supposing he had one, could raise his hand. Then "b" could raise his other hand, and "a" could raise his other hand, and we would have completed a cycle of communication by mimicry. Communication by mimicry could also be called communication in terms of mass.

We see that Reality is the degree of duplication between Cause and Effect. Affinity is monitored by intention and the particle sizes involved, as well as the distance. The greatest Affinity there is for anything is to occupy its same space. As the distance widens Affinity drops. Further, as the amount of mass or energy particles increases, so again does Affinity drop. Further, as the velocity departs from what "a" and "b" have considered optimum velocity—either greater or lesser velocity than what they consider to be the proper velocity—Affinity drops.

There is another fine point about communication, and that is expectancy.

Basically, all things are considerations. We consider that things are, and so they are. The idea is always senior to the mechanics of energy, space, time, mass. It would be possible to have entirely different ideas about communication than these. However, these happen to be the ideas of communication which are in common in this universe, and which are utilized by the life units of this universe. Here we have the basic agreement upon the subject of communication in the communication formula as given here. Because ideas are senior to this, a thetan can get, in addition to the communication formula, a peculiar idea concerning just exactly how communication should be conducted, and if this is not generally agreed upon, can find himself definitely out of communication. Let us take the example of a modernistic writer who insists that the first three letters of every word should be dropped, or that no sentence should be finished, or that the description of characters should be held to a cubist rendition. He will not attain agreement amongst his readers and so will become to some degree an "only one." There is a continuous action of natural selection, one might say, which weeds out strange or peculiar communication ideas. People, to be in communication, adhere to the basic rules as given here, and when anyone tries to depart too widely from these rules, they simply do not duplicate him and so, in effect, he goes out of communication.

We have seen an entire race of philosophers go out of existence since 1790. We have seen philosophy become a very unimportant subject, where once it was a very common coin amongst the people. The philosophers themselves put themselves out of communication with the people by insisting upon using words of special definitions which could not be assimilated with readiness by persons in general. The currency of philosophy could not be duplicated by those with relatively limited vocabularies. Take such jaw-cracking words as "telekinesis." While it probably means something very interesting and very vital, if you will think back carefully no taxi-driver mentioned this word to you while you were paying your fare, or even during the more verbose moments of the ride. Probably the basic trouble with philosophy was that it became Germanic in its grammar, an example set by Immanual Kant. And if you will recall that wonderful story by Saki, a man was once trampled to death while trying to teach an elephant German irregular verbs. Philosophy shed some of its responsibility for a cycle of communication by rendering itself unduplicatable by its readers. It is the responsibility of anyone who would communicate that he speak with such vocabulary as can be understood. Thus philosophy could not even begin for some hundred and fifty years a sound cycle of communication, and thus is dead.

Now let us take up the individual who has become very "experienced" in life. This individual has a time-track in particular. This time-track is his own time-track, it isn't anyone else's time-track. The basic individualities amongst men are based upon the fact that they have different things happen to them and that they view these different things from different points of view. Thus we have individualization and we have individual opinion, consideration and experience. Two men walking down the street witness an accident. Each one of them sees the accident from at least a slightly different point of view. Consulting twelve different witnesses to the same accident, we are likely to find twelve different accidents. Completely aside from the fact that witnesses like to tell you what they think they saw instead of what they saw, there were actually twelve different points from which the accident was viewed, and so twelve different aspects of the occurrences. If these twelve were brought together, and if they were to communicate amongst themselves about this accident, they would then reach a point of agreement on what actually happened. This might not have been the accident, but it certainly is the agreed-upon accident, which then becomes the real accident. This is the way juries conduct themselves. They might or might not be passing upon the real crime, but they are certainly passing upon the agreed-upon crime.

In any war it takes two or three days for enough agreement to occur to know what took place in a battle. Whereas there might have been a real battle, a real sequence of incidents and occurrences, the fact that every man in the battle saw the battle from his own particular point of view, by which we mean severely "point from which he was looking," rather than his opinions—no one saw the battle in its entirety. Thus, time must intervene for enough communication on the subject of the battle to take place so that all have some semblance of agreement on what occurred. Of course, when the historians get to this battle and start writing different accounts of it, out of the memoirs of generals who were trying to explain away their defeats, we get a highly distorted account indeed. And yet this becomes the agreed-upon battle, as far as history is concerned. Reading the historians one realizes that one will never really know what took place at Waterloo, at Bennington, at Marathon. In that we can consider as a communication one soldier shooting at another soldier, we see that we are studying communications about communication. This scholarly activity is all very nice, but does not carry us very far towards the resolution of human problems.

We have seen these two words "Cause" and "Effect" playing a prominent role in the communication formula. We have seen that First Cause became at the end of the cycle Last Effect. Furthermore, at the intermediate point, First Effect immediately changed to Cause in order to have a good communication cycle. What, then, do we mean by "Cause"? Cause is simply the point of emanation of the communication. What is "Effect"? Effect is the receipt point of the communication. In that we are only interested in life units, we see that we can readily ascertain cause at any time. We are not interested in secondary or tertiary Cause. We are not interested in assisting causes in any way. We are not interested in secondary or tertiary effects. We are not interested in assisting effects in any way. We consider any time that we look at a source point of a communication that we are looking at Cause. In that the entire track is composed of this pattern of Cause and Effect, an individual is very prone, whenever he sees a possible cause point, to look for an earlier cause point, and then an earlier one, and an earlier one, and an earlier one, and after a while takes to reading the Bible, which is very hard on the eyesight.

In view of the fact that all Cause is simply elected cause, and all Effect is simply elected effect, and that the primary echelon is the idea level of communication, that is Cause which we elect to be Cause, that is Effect which elects to be Effect, and there is no more that can be said about it. Cause in our dictionary here means only "source point." Effect means only "receipt point."

We notice that the receipt point, midway in the cycle of communication, shifts and becomes source point. We could classify this shift in the centre of the cycle of communication in some other fashion, but it is not necessary to do so. We would be getting too complicated for our purposes.

Now we come to the problem of what a life unit must be willing to experience in order to communicate. In the first place the primary cause point must be willing to be duplicatable. It must be able to give at least some attention to the receipt point. The primary receipt point must be willing to duplicate, must be willing to receive, and must be willing to change into a source point in order to send the communication, or an answer to it, back. And the primary source point in its turn must be willing to be a receipt point. As we are dealing basically with ideas and not mechanics, we see then that a state of mind must exist between a cause and effect point whereby each one is willing to be Cause or Effect at will, and is willing to duplicate at will, is willing to be duplicatable at will, is willing to change at will, is willing to experience the distance between, and, in short, willing to communicate. Where we get these conditions in an individual or a group we have sane people. Where an unwillingness to send or receive communications occurs, where people obsessively or compulsively send communications without direction and without trying to be duplicatable, where individuals in receipt of communications stand silent and do not acknowledge or reply, we have aberrative factors. And it is very interesting to note from the standpoint of processing, that we have all the aberrative factors there are. We do not need to know anything further about aberration than that it is a disarrangement of the cycle of communication. But to know that, of course, we have to know the component parts of communication and the expected behavior.

Some of the conditions which can occur in an aberrated line are a failure to be duplicatable before one emanates a communication, an intention contrary to being received, an unwillingness to receive or duplicate a communication, an unwillingness to experience distance, an unwillingness to change, an unwillingness to give attention, an unwillingness to express intention, an unwillingness to acknowledge, and, in general, an unwillingness to duplicate. We might go so far as to say that the reason communication takes place instead of occupying the same space and knowing—the communication introduces the idea of distance—is that one is unwilling to BE to the degree necessary to *be anything*. One would rather communicate than be. Thus we find that the inability to communicate is a gradient scale—it goes down along with the inability to be. We get individuals winding up as only willing to be themselves, whatever that is, and thus becoming "the only one." To the degree that a person becomes "the only one" he is unwilling to communicate on the remaining dynamics. An individual who has become only himself is in the sad and sorry plight of being off the Second, Third, and Fourth Dynamics, at least.

It might be seen by someone that the solution to communication is not to communicate. One might say that if he hadn't communicated in the first place he wouldn't be in trouble now. Perhaps there is some truth in this, but there is more truth in the fact that processing in the direction of making communication unnecessary, or reducing communication, is not processing at all, but murder. A man is as dead as he can't communicate. He is as alive as he can communicate. With countless tests in the Hubbard Association of Scientologists International department of writing and investigation, I have discovered to a degree which could be called conclusive, that the only remedy for livingness is further communicatingness. One must add to his ability to communicate.

Probably the only major error which exists in Eastern Philosophy, and probably the one at which I balked when I was young, was this idea that one should withdraw from life. It seemed to me that every good friend I had amongst the priests and holy men was seeking to pull back and cut off his communications with existence. Whatever the textbooks of Eastern Philosophy may say, this was the practice of the people who were best conversant with Eastern mental and spiritual know-how. Thus I saw individuals taking fourteen or eighteen years in order to get up to a high level of spiritualistic serenity. I saw a great many men studying and very few arriving. To my impatient and possibly practical Western viewpoint this was intolerable. For a very great many years I asked this question, "To communicate, or not to communicate?" If one got himself into such thorough trouble by communicating, then, of course, one should stop communicating. But this is not the case. If one gets himself into trouble by communicating, he should further communicate. More communication, not less, is the answer, and I consider this riddle solved after a quarter-century of investigation and pondering.

CHAPTER VIII

THE APPLICATION OF COMMUNICATION

If you think we are talking about anything very esoteric, or highly mathematical, kindly read the communication formula again. Just because we are speaking of the basic fundamentals of sanity, aberration, freedom, ability, truth, knowledge, and secrets is no reason why we have to be complicated. We expect the fundamentals of behaviour to be complicated simply because so many highly complicated people have discussed the subject. If Immanuel Kańt couldn't, and if Adler addled communication, there is no reason why we should.

As we speak of the applications of communication we are speaking of complexities of these fundamentals, and having isolated the fundamentals, we do not then see any complexity in the product of the basics. Let us say that we thoroughly understand that two plus two equals four. Now we write this on a piece of paper and put it on a table. It is still understandable. Now we write on another piece of paper that two plus two equals four and put it on the same table. Now on a third piece of paper we write two plus two equals four and add it to those on the table. We take four tablets full of paper and on each sheet we write two plus two equals four, and tearing each sheet out, add these. Now we get some blocks of wood, and we write two plus two equals four on these blocks of wood. We get some leather and charcoal and write two plus two equals four, and add that to the table. Then we get some blackboards, and on each one write two plus two equals four and put them on the table. And we get some coloured chalk and write two plus two equals four in various colours on another blackboard and put it on the table. Then we have two plus two equals four bound in vellum and add that to the pile on the table. Then we get some building bricks and we scratch on them two plus two equals four and put them on the table. Now we get four gallons of ink and pour it over two plus two equals four, and smear everything we've put on the table. Now we take a bulldozer and push the table out through the wall. We take a steam roller and run over the debris. We take some concrete and pour it over the whole and let it dry, and we still have not altered the fact that two plus two equals four.

In other words, no matter what mechanics we add to the communication formula, no matter what form we use to communicate, no matter how many types of words and meanings we place into the communication formula to become messages, no matter how we scramble meanings, messages, cause points and effect points, we still have a communication formula.

Here we have an individual. He has been living for a many-evented lifetime. He began life, let us say, with a perfect grasp of the communication formula. His experience has been a consistent departure from the communication formula only to the degree that he failed to emanate or failed to receive, twisted, perverted, or failed to return communications, and at the end of that lifetime all we have to do to put him into excellent condition would be to restore in its complete clarity his ability to execute the communication formula. The only thing which has happened to him has been violation of the communication formula. He emanated something. It was not received. When it was received it was not acknowledged. When it replied he did not receive it. And thus he begins to look further and further afield for communication and becomes more and more complicated in his view of communication and becomes less and less duplicatable, is less and less able to duplicate, his intentions swerve further and further, his attention becomes more and more altered, what should have been straight lines wind up in a ball, and we have our preclear after a lifetime of living with homo sapiens. All we have to do to get him into the most desirable clarity would be to restore his ability to perform the various parts of the communication formula and his ability to apply that formula to any thing in this or any universe. He would have to be willing to duplicate anything. He would have to be willing to make himself duplicatable. He would have to be able to tolerate distance and velocities and masses. He would have to be able to form his own intentions. He would have to be able to give and receive attention. He would have to be able to take or leave at will the intentions of others, and more important, he would have to be able to be at any point and make it cause or receipt point at will. If he were able to do this he could not possibly be trapped, for here we are intimately walking into the deepest secret of the trap.

What is a secret? It is the answer which was never given, and this is all a secret is. Thus knowledge and use of the communication formula within the framework of Dianetics and Scientology resolves any and all secrets and even the belief in secrets.

The only thing that could be said to aberrate communication would be restriction, or fear of restriction. A person who is not communicating is one who has restricted communication. A person who is communicating compulsively is afraid of being restricted in his communication. A person who is talking on another subject than that to which Cause was giving his attention has been so restricted on the subject of communication elsewhere, or has experienced such a scarcity of communication elsewhere, that he is still involved with communication elsewhere. This is what we mean by "not in present time."

When we look at problems without which humanity cannot seem to live we discover that a problem is no more and no less than a confusion of communication lines, missing cause or effect points, undeterminable distances, misread intentions, missing attention, and failures in the ability to duplicate and be duplicatable. Move off the communication formula in any direction and a problem will result. A problem, by definition, is something without an answer, not because the two words are similar, but because all of humanity has confused them. We find that answer to a communication and answer to a problem can, for our purposes, be synonymous.

When one has failed to get answers consistently to his communications, he begins to run into a scarcity of answers, and he will get problems in order to have solutions, but he will not solve any of the problems because he already has a scarcity of answers. An auditor walks in on a preclear who has a scarcity of answers, finds the preclear has a circuit of problems, tries to resolve some of the problems of the preclear, discovers that the preclear creates new problems faster than old ones can be resolved. One thing the preclear knows is that there aren't any answers—not for his particular kind of problems. He knows this is to such a degree that he is unable to conceive of answers, which means to him that he is unable to conceive of solutions. He is like the old man in Manuel Komroff's story who, after his release from prison, yet created a cell of his own. He cannot look at freedom. He does not believe freedom exists. He cannot envision a world without tigers. The remedy for this, of course, is to have him remedy his lack of answers by having him mock up answers.

That confused look you see on a mathematician's face is the task he has set himself to procure symbolic answers to hypothetical abstracts, none of which, of course, are human answers. The longer he symbolizes, the more formulas he creates, the further he drifts from the human race. Answers are answers only when they come from living units. All else is a glut on the market. No mathematical formula ever gave anybody any answer to anything unless it was to the problem of communication itself, but this I'll invite to your attention, was not involved with, and was not derived from, mathematics as we know them. The communication formula was derived from an observation of and working with life. It could be derived only because one had entirely abandoned the idea that energy could tell anyone anything. Life is not energy. Energy is the by-product of Life.

Your recluse is one who has become so thoroughly convinced that there are no obtainable answers from anyone that he does no longer believe that Life itself exists. He is the only living thing alive, in his opinion. Why? Because he is the only thing which communicates. I daresay every recluse, every "only one," every obsessively or compulsively communicating individual has so thoroughly associated with "life units" which were so dead that it became "very plain" that no one else was alive. The attitude of a child towards the adult contains the opinion that adults have very little Life in them. A child, with his enthusiasms, is in his family everywhere surrounded by communication blocks of greater or lesser magnitude. His questions do not get answers. The communications which are addressed to him are not posed in a way which can be duplicated. In other words, the adult does not make himself duplicatable. Freud and his confreres were entirely in error in believing that the child is totally self-centred. It is not the child who is totally self-centred. He believes that he is in communication with the total world. Investigation of children demonstrates that they are very heavy on the First, Second, Third and Fourth Dynamics. The child is so convinced of his ability to communicate that he will touch a hot stove. Life has no terrors for him. He has not yet learned by experience that he cannot communicate. It's the adult who is drawn back into the "only one" and one believes that the inspiration of this continuous belief on the part of a psychologist and psychoanalyst that the child is entirely self-centred and has only his own world must be the expression of an opinion held by the psychoanalyst and psychologist out of his own bank. As one grows one goes less and less into communication with the environment until he is at last entirely out of it. Only he is out of it in the wrong direction—dead.

Where you see aberration, where you would wish to detect aberration, you must look for violations in the communication formula. People who consistently and continually violate portions of the communication formula can be suspected of being just that dead. The further one departs from the communication formula the more death exists for them. The more concentrated they become on secrets, the more they question intentions, the less they are likely to assume the point of view called Cause or the point of view called Effect.

One should not go so far as to say that Life is communication. It is, however, a native condition of Life to be able to communicate. Life, the awareness of awareness unit, the ability to have unlimited quality with no quantity, or to produce quantity, is capable of communication. And here again we are consulting ability. Ability, first and foremost, could be conceived to be the ability to BE, and also the ability to vary being, and this means the ability to communicate. One has to be able to *be* in order to communicate. One has to be able to vary one's beingness in order to return communication.

There is the manifestation, then, known as the "stuck flow." This is one-way communication. The flow can be stuck incoming or it can be stuck outgoing. The part of a communication cycle that goes from primary Cause to Effect may be the flow that is stuck, or it might be the other from "b" back to "a" that is stuck. Here we have several possible methods of achieving a stuck flow, and several conditions of flow, four to be exact. The flow can be stuck from primary Cause to Effect, from the viewpoint of primary Cause. The flow can be stuck from primary Cause to primary Effect from the viewpoint of primary Effect. The flow can be stuck from Effect-turned-Cause to final Effect, from the viewpoint of Effect-turned-Cause. The flow can be stuck from Effect-turned-Cause to final Effect, from the viewpoint of final Effect. These four stuck flows can become — any of them or a combination of them — the anatomy of a communication lag of a case. A person can hear but cannot answer. A person can cause a communication to begin, but cannot receive an acknowledgement. A primary Cause can be totally engrossed in keeping the flow from arriving at primary Effect, etc.

A failure to complete a cycle of communication will leave some part of that communication in suspense. It will leave it, in other words, silent, and this will stick on the track. It will float in time. It will restimulate. It will attract and hold attention long after it occurred.

Unconsciousness itself results from the receipt of too much, too heavy, communication. It can similarly, but less often, result from the emanation of too much, too heavy, communication as in the case of blowing up a large balloon, where one becomes dizzy after the expulsion of too much breath. Theoretically, one sending a large mass towards another might fall unconscious as a result of sending too much mass away from himself too suddenly, and we find that this can be the case. This is degradation because of loss. One gives away too much, or loses too much, and the departure of the mass, or even the idea, can bring about a drop in consciousness. In view of the fact that a thetan can create at will this is not a very dangerous situation. One can receive too much communication too suddenly, such as a cannon ball. Unconsciousness will result from this. Most engrams are composed of too much incoming mass and too much outgoing mass, so as to make a confusion into which any answer, any phrase interjected can then be effective since there is a scarcity of phrases and a plus in masses. One could even go so far as to say that the only reason a mass interchange is ever effective in the line of unconsciousness is that it does not have enough reasons with it. I suppose that if one explained carefully enough to a soldier why he had to be shot, the arrival of a bullet would not make him unconscious or hurt him. But again this is theoretical, as very little reason goes on in war, thus it has never been subjected to a clinical experiment.

The resolution of any stuck flow is remedying the scarcity of that which stuck the flow. This might be answers, it might be original communication, it might be chances to reply.

The communication formula at work is best understood through the "communication lag."

CHAPTER IX

TWO-WAY COMMUNICATION

A cycle of communication and two-way communication are actually two different things. If we examine closely the anatomy of communication we will discover that a cycle of communication is not a two-way communication in its entirety.

If you will inspect Graph "A" below, you will see a cycle of communication :

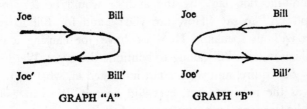

GRAPH "A"   GRAPH "B"

Here we have Joe as the originator of a communication. It is his primary impulse. This impulse is addressed to Bill. We find Bill receiving it, and then Bill originating an answer or acknowledgement as Bill', which acknowledgement is sent back to Joe'. Joe has said, for instance, "How are you?" Bill has received this, and then Bill (becoming secondary Cause) has replied to it as Bill', with "I'm O.K.," which goes back to Joe', and thus ends the cycle.

Now what we call a two-way cycle of communication may ensue, as in Graph "B."

Here we have Bill originating a communication. Bill says, "How's tricks?" Joe receives this, and then as Joe' or secondary Cause, answers "O.K., I guess," which answer is then acknowledged in its receipt by Bill'.

In both of these graphs we discover that in Graph "A" the acknowledgement of the secondary Cause was expressed by Joe' as a nod or a look of satisfaction. And again, in Graph "B," Joe's' "O.K., I guess" is actually acknowledged by Bill' with a nod or some expression signifying receipt of the communication.

If both Joe and Bill are "strong, silent men"—highly aberrated—they would omit some portion of these cycles. The most flagrant omission and the one most often understood as "communication lag" by the auditor would be for Joe in Graph "A" to say "How are you?" and for Bill to stand there without speaking. Here we have Joe causing a communication, and Bill failing to continue the cycle. We do not know or require, and we are not interested in, whether or not Bill, as the receipt point, ever did hear it. We can assume that he was at least present, and that Joe spoke loudly enough to be heard, and that Bill's attention was somewhere in Joe's vicinity. Now instead of getting on with the cycle of communication, Joe is left there with an incompleted cycle and never gets an opportunity to become Joe'.

There are several ways in which a cycle of communication could not be completed, and these could be categorized as (1) Joe failing to emanate communication, (2) Bill failing to hear communication, (3) Bill' failing to reply to the communication received by him, and (4) Joe' failing to acknowledge by some sign or word that he has heard Bill'.

We could assign various reasons to all this, but our purpose here is not to assign reasons why we do not complete a communication cycle. Our entire purpose is involved with the non-completion of this communication cycle.

Now, as in Graph "A," let us say we have in Joe a person who is compulsively and continually originating communication whether he has anybody's attention or not, and whether or not these communications are germane to any existing situation. We discover that Joe is apt to be met, in his communicating, with an inattentive Bill who does not hear him, and thus an absent Bill' who does not answer, and thus an absent Joe' who never acknowledges.

Let us examine this same situation in Graph "B." Here we have, in Bill, an origination of a communication. We have the same Joe with a compulsive outflow. Bill says, "How are you?" and the cycle is not completed because Joe, so intent upon his own compulsive line, does not become Joe' and never gives Bill a chance to become Bill' and acknowledge.

Now let's take another situation. We find Joe originating communications, and Bill a person who never originates communications. Joe is not necessarily compulsive or obsessive in originating communications, but Bill is aberratedly inhibited in originating communications. We find that Joe and Bill, working together, then get into this kind of an activity: Joe originates a communication, Bill hears it, becomes Bill', replies to it, and permits Joe a chance to become Joe'. This goes on quite well, but will sooner or later hit a jam on a two-way cycle, which is violated because Bill never originates communications.

A two-way cycle of communication would work as follows: Joe, having originated a communication, and having completed it, may then wait for Bill to originate a communication to Joe, thus completing the remainder of the two-way cycle of communication. Bill does originate a communication, this is heard by Joe, answered by Joe', and acknowledged by Bill'.

Thus we get the normal cycle of a communication between two terminals, for in this case Joe is a terminal and Bill is a terminal and communication can be seen to flow between two terminals. The cycles depend on Joe originating communication, Bill hearing the communication, Bill becoming Bill' and answering the communication, Joe' acknowledging the communication, then Bill originating a communication, Joe hearing the communication, Joe' answering the communication, and Bill' acknowledging the communication. If they did this, regardless of what they were talking about, they would never become in an argument and would eventually reach an agreement, even if they were hostile to one another. Their difficulties and problems would be cleared up and they would be, in relationship to each other, in good shape.

A two-way communication cycle breaks down when either terminal fails, in its turn, to originate communication. We discover that the entire society has vast difficulties along this line. They are so used to canned entertainment and so inhibited in originating communication by parents who couldn't communicate, and by education and other causes, that people get very low on communication origin. Communication origin is necessary to start a communication in the first place. Thus we find people talking mainly about things which are forced upon them by exterior causes. They see an accident, they discuss it. They see a movie, they discuss it. They wait for an exterior source to give them the occasion for a conversation. But in view of the fact that both are low on the origin of communication—which could also be stated as low on imagination—we discover that such people, dependent upon exterior primal impulses, are more or less compulsive or inhibitive in communication, and thus the conversation veers rapidly and markedly and may wind up with some remarkable animosities or mis-conclusions. Let us suppose that lack of prime cause impulse on Joe's part has brought him into obsessive or compulsive communication, and we find that he is so busy outflowing that he never has a chance to hear anyone who speaks to him, and if he did hear them would not answer them. Bill on the other hand, might be so very, very, very low on primal cause (which is to say, low on communication origination) that he never even moves into Bill', or if he does, would never put forth his own opinion, thus unbalancing Joe further and further into further and further compulsive communication.

As you can see by these graphs, some novel situations could originate. There would be the matter of obsessive answering as well as inhibitive answering. An individual could spend all of his time answering, justifying or explaining—all the same thing—no primal communication having been originated at him. Another individual, as Joe' in Graph "A" or Bill' in Graph "B," might spend all of his time acknowledging, even though nothing came his way to acknowledge. The common and most noticed manifestations, however, are obsessive and compulsive origin, and non-answering acceptance, and non-acknowledgement of answer. And at these places we can discover stuck flows.

As the only crime in the universe seems to be to communicate, and as the only saving grace of a thetan is to communicate, we can readily understand that an entanglement of communication is certain to result, but we can understand—and much more happily—that it can now be resolved.

That which we are discussing here is minimally theory and maximally derived from observation. The main test of this is whether or not it resolved cases, and be assured that it does.

Flows become stuck on this twin cycle of communication where a scarcity occurs in (1) origination of communication, (2) receipt of communication, (3) answering of communication given, (4) acknowledging answers. Thus it can be seen that there are only four parts which can become aberrated in both Graph "A" and Graph "B," no matter the number of peculiar manifestations which can occur as a result thereof.

These observations of communications are so vital that a considerable difference amongst case results comes about between an auditor who does acknowledge whatever his preclear answers and an auditor who does not. Let us take "Auditor G" and we discover that he is running Opening Procedure of 8-C on a preclear, but that at the end of two hours of Opening Procedure of 8-C the preclear has benefited very little. Then let us take "Auditor K." This auditor does 15 minutes of Opening Procedure of 8-C and gets very good results on the preclear. The difference between Auditor G and Auditor K is only that Auditor G never acknowledges any answer or statement, or communication origin on the part of the preclear. He simply continues doggedly with the process. Auditor K. on the other hand, is willing to let the preclear originate a communication and always acknowledges whenever the preclear concludes the action called for in a command. or when the preclear volunteers a verbal answer. In other words. G did not answer or acknowledge—but ran the process with mechanical perfection, and K both answered and acknowledged as well as originated orders. The fact that the scarcest thing there is is the origin of orders or communications, and the fact that G was at least doing this, was enough to cause G to get some improvement in the preclear, but he would not get anything like the improvement obtained by Auditor K.

Silence is nowhere desirable except in permitting another to communicate or waiting for another to acknowledge. The auditing of silence will wind the preclear in a perfect fish-net of aberration. The total process which remedies this is remedying the scarcity, by whatever means, of the four parts of a two-way communication.

CHAPTER X

COMMUNICATION LAG

Yesterday we used an instrument called an E-Meter to register whether or not the process was still getting results so that the auditor would know how long to continue it. While the E-Meter is an interesting investigation instrument and has played its part in research, it is not today used by the auditor except perhaps in testing the basal metabolism of the preclear. The E-Meter is no longer used to determine "what is wrong with the preclear." As we long ago suspected, the intervention of a mechanical gadget between the auditor and the preclear had a tendency to de-personalize the session and also gave the auditor a dependence upon the physical universe and its meters which did not have to be there. I knew when we first began to use E-Meters that sooner or later something would have to be evolved, or that something would turn up which would dispense with them. I worked along that line rather consistently and about half a year before this writing developed "communication lag" as the only diagnostic instrument needed by the auditor.*

The exact definition of a communication lag is: "the length of time intervening between the posing of a question, or origination of a statement, and the exact moment that question or original statement is answered."

* The Mark V E-Meter, though not a diagnostic instrument, was developed by L. Ron Hubbard since this writing for precision auditing.

If you will look very closely at this definition you will discover that nothing is said, whatever, about what goes on between the asking of the question or the origination of a communication and its being answered. What goes on in between is lag. It does not matter if the preclear stood on his head, went to the North Pole, gave a dissertation on Botany, stood silent, answered some other question, thought it over, attacked the auditor, or began to string beads. Any other action but answering, and the time taken up by that action, is communication lag. An auditor has to understand this very thoroughly. Usually he interprets a communication lag as the length of time it takes the preclear to answer the question and loosely applies this as the length of time between the asking of the question and the first moment the preclear starts to speak. This is not communication lag, for the preclear may start to speak on some other subject, may desire information, may *almost* answer the question, and still not actually answer the question.

If you will look around at people you will find them possessed of a great many communication lag mechanisms. In their effort not to be an effect, or in their effort not to be cause, in their aberrations about compulsive communication, and inhibitive communication, and in indulging in impulsive, compulsive and inhibitive communication they manage to assemble quite a number of interesting mechanisms. But all these mechanisms are communication lag.

Here is an example of communication lag. Joe: "How are you, Bill?" Bill: "You look fine, Joe." Here the question was never answered at all and would go on as a communication lag from there until the end of the universe.

Here is another example: Joe: "How are you, Bill?" Bill

(after twenty seconds of study): "Oh, I guess I'm all right today." As this is the commonest form of communication lag it is the most readily observed.

Less well known is the following communication lag. Joe: "How are you, Bill?" Bill: "What do you want to know for?" Again, this question goes on unanswered until the end of the universe.

The most maddening kind of communication lag is, Joe: "How are you Bill?" Bill:——silence from there on out. This is dramatized when people anxiously inquire of an unconscious person how he is and they become entirely frantic. They are simply looking at a communication lag which they believe will become total, and their anxiety is simply their multiple suffering on the subject of communication lag.

Here is another type of communication lag. Joe: "How are you, Bill? I was saying to Ezra the other day that I have seen a lot of sick men in my time, but you certainly look pretty bad. Bill, now how are you? I've been down to see the doctor and he was telling me there's a lot of these colds and things going around . . ." In other words, Joe never gives Bill an opportunity to reply, and this is the other side of communication lag.

An auditor's understanding of the subject of communication lag is brief if he believes it is the lag between the originator of the communication and the person to whom it is addressed. On our Graph "A" on an earlier page this would be from Joe to Bill'. There is a return lag, and that is from Bill' to Joe', and, as above, there is a lag between Joe and Joe' where Joe simply keeps on talking without ascertaining if there is any Bill' there. You could also call this return lag an "acknowledgement lag." Joe to Joe is not a communication at all. Actually, Joe to Bill' without the completion of the cycle is the same thing. Joe never acknowledges a communication and so the return lag is actually Joe to Joe. The proper sequence of such a communication is Bill' to Joe'. In other words Joe, to make a complete cycle of communication, must acknowledge in some manner, verbal or gesture, that Bill' has said something.

Joe to Joe, as a communication lag (which is to say, no acknowledgement) has as its initial root an absence, for Joe, of Bill to Bill' in Graph "B." In other words, Joe has been called upon to originate communication so consistently that he now does so compulsively and obsessively since there has been an entire scarcity of other people originating communication.

Now let us look at a highly specialized type of communication lag. Here we have Joe to Bill to Bill' to Joe', as in Graph "A." Then we have Joe waiting for Bill, in Graph "B," to originate a communication. If Bill does not, and only silence ensues, Joe then originates another communication. In other words, we have no two-way communication.

The two-way cycle of communication is not quite as important in auditing as it would be in Life, for in auditing the auditor perforce is originating communication in order to get the preclear up to the point where he can originate communication. One does not remedy Life by approximating it exactly in the auditing room. The process is so designed that it will accomplish a rehabilitation in Life without, to a marked degree, having to live it. As an example of this, the auditor does not expect the preclear to turn around and originate some process to make the auditor well. But the auditor does expect to get audited by somebody sooner or later, or expects to be at a level where he can rise above this need of a communication interchange in order to live.

The place auditors have the most trouble with the communication lag is the return lag. Auditors seldom acknowledge the execution of commands on the part of the preclear. As in Opening Procedure of 8-C, a process which is one of the six basic processes, the auditor sends the preclear over to touch the wall. When the preclear has touched the wall, the auditor is quite prone to give another command without acknowledging the fact that the preclear has touched the wall. It is an amazing thing what the lack of acknowledgement will do to slow down a case recovery. Many times when an auditor is doing this acknowledging, he is doing it in such a perfunctory fashion that the preclear does not recognize it as an acknowledgement, but as a prelude to a new command. A good auditor makes very, very sure that the preclear knows the acknowledgement has occurred. As an example, the auditor says: "Go over to the wall and touch it." The preclear does so. The auditor says: "Very good," and with a definite pause after this acknowledgement says: "Now go over to that wall and touch it." In other words, the auditor who is a good auditor makes sure that the preclear knows that a complete cycle of communication has occurred on this particular auditing command.

Another failure on the part of auditors is to fail to let the preclear originate a communication. The auditor tells the preclear: "Go over to that wall and touch it." The preclear does so but stops midway in the gesture and gasps, then completes the gesture. The bad auditor will fail to note and inquire after this gasp. This is actually the origin of a communication on the part of the preclear. He does not verbalize it. He does not express it any further than some physical gesture or a look of dismay, and even these might be slight, but this is usually as far as he can go in originating a communication. The auditor who fails to pick this up fails to inform the preclear thus that the preclear is permitted to originate a communication. This gasp, this gesture, should at once be noted by the auditor with a "What's happened?" or, "What's the matter?" or, "Something happen?" This gives the preclear the opportunity to originate a second cycle of communication. Remember that the gesture or the gasp was actually a communication. The preclear probably will not acknowledge the auditor's statement beyond starting out on the origin of a new communication, but the fact that he does originate a statement on the subject of what is the matter is, in itself, an acknowledgement of the fact that he has heard the auditor. This is so vital that many cases have stumbled, tripped, and bogged, simply because the auditor did not encourage the preclear to make a statement as to something which had occurred. Actually, the more often an auditor can do this the better auditor he is, and the more good will be done by auditing.

Now, of course, there is an opposite side of this where the auditor can give credence to an obsessive or compulsive outflow on the part of the preclear to such an extent that the auditing is entirely interrupted. An example of this occurred recently where a preclear outflowed at an auditor three days and three nights without the auditor recognizing entirely that this was simply obsessive communication in action. But this is not communication. This is not pertinent to the situation, and the definition of compulsive or obsessive communication is "an outflow which is not pertinent to the surrounding terminals and situation." In other words, compulsive or obsessive communication is an outflow which is not in reality with the existing reality.

We see, then, that an auditing session really does include two-way cycle of communication, but it does not include it, ever, unless the auditor invites the preclear to comment upon what is going on as he does processes.

Just as a side comment here, the way to handle an obsessive or a compulsive communication is to wait for a slight break in the flow and interject an auditing command. Remember that an obsessive outflow is actually not a communication. A communication is on the subject and is in agreement with the environment. It is also in agreement with what is occurring.

Now it doesn't happen to matter what process is being done, the basic of that process is two-way communication. In auditing, as in living, communication is existence. In the absence of communication we have silence, and where we have silence we have no time. Time is manifested in communication lag to the extent that the preclear has been subjected to silences, or such a thing as an obsessive or compulsive outflow which had nothing to do with communicating on the subject at hand. This is again a sort of silence — somebody talking obsessively or continually about things which might or might not exist, and to no one in particular without expecting any cycle of communication to take place.

A communication lag is handled by an auditor by repetition of a question or command which elicited a communication lag. Here is an example. Bill: "How are you, Joe?" Joe: silence; silence; silence — finally a grunt. Bill: "How are you, Joe?" Joe: silence, silence — "O.K., I guess." Bill: "How are you, Joe?" Joe: "I'm all right, I tell you!" Bill: "How are you, Joe?" Joe: silence — "I'm O.K." Bill: "How are you Joe?" Joe: "All right, I guess." Bill: "How are you, Joe?" Joe:

"All right." Bill: "How are you Joe?" Joe: "Oh, I'm all right."

This is an example of flattening a communication lag.* At first we have silence and no very intelligible reply, then we have silence and a reply, and then other manifestations, each one of which demonstrates a changing interval of time until the last couple of commands—three, in actual auditing practice—where the same interval of time was present.

Flattening a communication lag requires only that the preclear answer after a uniform interval of time at least three times. This uniform interval of time could, for practical purposes, be as long as 10 seconds. Thus we get lengths of time required to answer an auditing question as follows: answer requires 35 seconds; answer requires 20 seconds; answer requires 45 seconds; answer requires 20 seconds; answer requires 10 seconds; answer requires 10 seconds; answer requires 10 seconds. To all intents and purposes, with these three last 10 second intervals the auditor could consider that he has to some degree flattened this particular auditing command because he is getting a consistent response. However, with such a long lag as 10 seconds, the auditor will discover that if he asked the question two or three more times he would recover a changing interval once more.

This is the mechanical formula of flattening communication lag. Give the order, as in Opening Procedure of 8-C, or ask the question, as in Straightwire, and then continue to give that same order or ask that same question until the preclear executes it after a short interval three times the same.

There is an entirely different manifestation for a comple-

* Note that this is an example only, not an actual process or question an auditor would use repetitively.—Ed.

tely flattened communication lag. We get extroversion. The preclear ceases to put his attention on his mind, but puts his attention on the environment. We see this happen often in the Opening Procedure of 8-C where the preclear has the room suddenly become bright to him. He has extroverted his attention. He has come free from one of these communication tangles out of the past and has suddenly looked at the environment. This is all that has happened. On a thinkingness level this happens quite often. The preclear is doing the process very well, and then begins to remember odds and ends of appointments he has, or some such thing. Just because he does this is no reason the auditing session should be ended. It simply demonstrates an extroversion. You have, in one way or another, pulled the preclear out of a communication tangle and put him into present time, when he extroverts.

Communication lag as a subject could be a very large one. We have all manner of communication lags in evidence around us. Probably the most interesting one is the shock reaction after an accident, which one occasionally sees. At times it takes the body 36 hours to find out and reply to the fact that it has received an impact. It is quite common for a body to suddenly manifest the impact half an hour after it. This is communication lag. There are many humorous angles to communication lag. Sometimes you ask somebody "How are you?" and you get a reply from his social machinery. He says, "I'm fine." Then, two or three hours later, he is liable to say to you, "I feel terrible." This was the preclear, himself, answering. This was the awareness of awareness unit awakening to this communication lag.

This universe could be called a consistent and continuous communication lag. One is trapped in it to the degree that he is lagging. If there were no remedy for communication lag I would never bring up the subject. However, there is, and it is a remedy which is easily undertaken in auditing today.

Entrapment is actually communication lag. One has waited for communication which never arrived, expected something to answer so long and so often that he becomes fixated upon something, or in somethings, and so does not believe he can escape from it. The first and foremost factor in communication lag, of course, is time, and the next factor is waiting which is also dependent upon time.

As has been commented earlier, the only things which float on the time track are the moments of silence when no communication occurred. These are "no time" moments, and so have no time in which they can live, and so they float forward on the time-track. It is an oddity that an engram behaves in such a way as to put all its silent moments in present time with the preclear and leave its talking or action moments back on the track. When we took a person back to birth and ran out birth, we took out the action moments. If we did not take out, as well, the silent moments in birth, we did not take out the very things which pin themselves to the preclear in present time. In other words, the birth engram did not move at all, but the silent moments in birth might have a tendency to come up into present time. These silent moments in engrams and facsimiles do, themselves, compose the matter extant in the preclear. This matter is not so much composed of action moments as silent moments. Thus we see that an individual, the longer he lives in this universe, the more communication lag he runs into, the more upset he is about existence, the greater his communication lag, the more he is silent. Of course, obsessive or compulsive communication is just one grade above silence. It is the last frantic effort to keep things from going entirely quiet. It is not communication and is actually silence of a sort, particularly since very few people listen to it.

Now we are studying about communication, and we are communicating about communication, and you have every opportunity here to get yourself beautifully snarled, so I would ask you to look around your environment and check a number of manifestations of communication lag. You are not controlled by the subject. You can easily control it. The dangerous thing is not to know the answers and simply go on in these consistent and continual communication lags imposed upon us by the lack of communication in this universe.

It is of great interest to note that imagination as a function of existence becomes drowned in an absence of communication origin. An individual can become so dependent upon others or entertainments in originating communications that he himself does not. Indeed, it is very unpopular in this society at this time to originate communications. One should always say that somebody else thought of it first, or that it goes back to the ancient Ugluks, or that it's happened many times before, or that one has just dug up the information after it has been buried, or one is really taking directions from the Archangel Smearel, rather than stand up and plead guilty to originating a communication. Unless one can originate communications one's imagination is in bad shape. The reverse does not happen to be true. The imagination is not that thing which is first imperilled and then results in failure to originate communication. Failure of communication origin then results in failure of imagination, so the rehabilitation of communication origin rehabilitates as well the imagination.

This is very good news, indeed, for anyone in the creative arts, particularly, but who is not in the creative arts?

Examining the whole subject of communication one discovers that there are very few people around him in this day and age who are actually communicating, and there are a lot of people who think they are communicating who are not.

CHAPTER XI

PAN-DETERMINISM

An entirely new concept in Dianetics and Scientology is that of Pan-Determinism.

In Book One we talked about Self-Determinism. Self-Determinism meant, in essence, control by the awareness of awareness unit of that which it conceived to be its identity. Some effort was made in Book One to move Self-Determinism out into the remaining Dynamics.

Pan-Determinism is a word which describes determinism all along the Dynamics. Actually, Self-Determinism attempted to do this, and our earlier idea of Self-Determinism was a sort of Pan-Determinism.

We have to remember here that the Dynamics involved in Dianetics are the first four. The Dynamics involved in Scientology are the last four of the total set of eight. The Eight Dynamics are as follows:

DYNAMIC ONE is the urge towards survival of self.

DYNAMIC TWO is the urge towards survival through sex, or children, and embraces both the sexual act and the care and raising of children.

DYNAMIC THREE is the urge towards survival through the group and as the group.

DYNAMIC FOUR is the urge towards survival through all mankind and as all mankind.

DYNAMIC FIVE is the urge towards survival through life forms such as animals, birds, insects, fish and vegetation, and is the urge to survive as these.

DYNAMIC SIX is the urge towards survival as the physical universe and has as its components Matter, Energy, Space and Time, from which we derive the word MEST.

DYNAMIC SEVEN is the urge towards survival through Spirit and would include the manifestations or the totality of awareness of awareness units, thetans, demons, ghosts, spirits, goblins, and so forth.

DYNAMIC EIGHT is the urge towards survival through a Supreme Being, or more exactly, Infinity. It is called Dynamic Eight because it is Infinity turned up on its side.

The urge towards survival through self, sex, children, groups and mankind is the proper province of Dianetics.

Now let us examine the concept of Pan-Determinism. Pan-Determinism would be the willingness to determine or control self and dynamics, other than self, up to the eight listed above. Like Self-Determinism, Pan-Determinism is self-elected or self-determined, in that one does it knowingly and directly, not from obsession, compulsion or inhibition. An undetermined individual, of course, does not exist, but an other-determined individual definitely can exist. Where we have Self-Determinism, and we interpret Self-Determinism as determinism on the First Dynamic, we have only willingness to control self and no willingness to control anything beyond self. If this is the case, in Self-Determinism we have as other-determinism sex, children, groups, mankind, and going on into Scientology, animal life, vegetation, the physical universe, spirits, and God—or whatever else might compose Infinity. In view of the fact that Self-Determinism was interpreted in this fashion it left an individual in the state of mind of being willing to be determined on all other Dynamics and by all other Dynamics except his own personal dynamic. In view of the fact that all auditing is the Third Dynamic, and in view of the fact that a personal dynamic cannot exist, and that an individual as we see him, a man, is actually a composite and is not a First Dynamic but a Third Dynamic, we see we are in difficulty with this definition of Self-Determinism and continued use of Self-Determinism. It is necessary, then, to investigate further and to assign more precision to this concept of willingness to control.

When we say control we do not mean the "control case" where control is obsessive or other-determined, or where the individual is controlling things out of compulsion or fear. We simply mean willingness to start, stop and change. The anatomy of control is just that—starting, stopping and changing things. Now it is not necessary for a person to start, stop and change things just to demonstrate that he can control them. He must, however, to be healthy and capable, be able to start, stop and change things.

Here we come immediately to what we mean by ability. It would be the ability to start, change and stop things, and if we have an ability to start, stop and change things, we of course must have a willingness to start, stop and change things. Those people who are unwillingly behaving in some direction so as to start, stop and change things are very sick people, and in this last category we discover the bulk of the human race at this writing.

The basic difference between aberration and sanity, between inability and ability, between illness and health, is the knowingness of causation by self opposed to unknown causation by others or other things. An individual who knows he is doing it is far more capable than one who is doing it but supposes something else is doing it. Psychosis is itself simply an inversion of determinism. A psychotic is entirely other-determined, a sane man is in good measure Self-Determined. Pan-Determinism would mean a willingness to start, change and stop on any and all dynamics. That is its primary definition. A further definition, also a precision definition, is: the willingness to start, change and stop two or more forces, whether or not opposed, and this could be interpreted as two or more individuals, two or more groups, two or more planets, two or more life-species, two or more universes, two or more spirits, whether or not opposed. This means that one would not necessarily fight, he would not necessarily choose sides.

This is in total controversy to some of the most cherished beliefs of Man, but may I point out to you quickly that Man is not an entirely sane person, and thus some of his beliefs must be somewhat aberrated. There is such a thing as courage, but there is not such a thing as sanity totally opposed.

People who are afraid of control are liable to be afraid of Pan-Determinism but if they will see this as a willingness to start, change and stop any Dynamic they will see that a person must be assuming the responsibility for any of the Dynamics. A conqueror, in his onslaught against society, is fighting other-determinism. He is starting, changing and stopping things because of an unwillingness to associate with or support other races or customs than his own. Therefore, what he is doing can be interpreted as "bad."

In support of this we get all of the earlier religious teachings, but these have been grossly misinterpreted. These have been interpreted to mean that a person should not fight in any way, or defend anything, or have anything, or own anything. This is not true. A person who is willing to be other identities besides himself, other individualities besides himself, does not necessarily harm these other individualities. Indeed, we cannot make the complete distinction of other than himself, since we are saying in this that he clings to something he calls self and supports and defends it without being willing to identify himself with others.

One of the most maddening debaters is one who moves at will between the viewpoints of himself and those who have elected him as an enemy.

There is an important scale down from Pan-Determinism. It does not lead along a dwindling Dynamic path, but it could, of course. One could simply see as Pan-Determinism dwindling the falling off of one Dynamic after another until one is down to First Dynamic, but that is not a particularly workable picture and an auditor does not use it.

The Scale down from Pan-Determinism is: Pan-Determinism, Fighting, Must and Must Not Happen Again, Repair and Association. These are actually processes. At the bottom we find an unwillingness to associate with anything. Just above this is an unwillingness to repair anything, but a willingness to associate somewhat. Above this is a willingness to associate and to repair somewhat, but no willingness to let certain things happen again. Above this is a willingness to fight things, and above this is Pan-Determinism. These are arranged in this fashion because this is the ladder a preclear climbs if he is run on a certain type of process. This is something like the old Emotional Scale, which went: Apathy, Grief, Fear, Anger, Antagonism, Boredom, Conservatism, and Enthusiasm, only in this case it is a scale of behaviour manifestations. Where an individual who is unwilling to associate with various things is certainly a long way from being Pan-Determined and definitely is not even Self-Determined, he has to come up a ways before he is willing to repair anything, but in this frame of mind he can repair quite generally but is unwilling or unable to create or destroy. An oddity here is that a person who is unwilling to associate is only able to destroy, and a person has to be very far up the scale before he can create. In fact, he has to be up around Pan-Determinism to adequately create. Above this level of repair we find an individual frozen in many incidents which he is preventing from occurring once more and is holding the facsimiles or engrams of these incidents so that he will have a model and so know what mustn't occur; and above this level we discover an individual fighting and being willing to fight almost anything; and above this level we discover an individual willing or able to be almost anything and so may be at peace with things and does not have to fight things. An individual at the Pan-Determinism level can create. An individual at Association, as I have said, can only destroy. An individual at Repair or Must and Must Not Happen Again is making a very, very heavy effort—and I do mean Effort—to survive.

Let us take for our example of Pan-Determinism the Second Dynamic. Here we find such a thorough effort to have other-determinism that Freud picked this out as the only aberrative factor. It is not the only aberrative factor, but in view of the fact that it is a desired inflow it can be considered with many other things to have some aberrative value. Let us look at it in terms of Self-Determinism and Pan-Determinism. Here we have an individual believing himself to be a man, who believes that his only sexual pleasure can be derived from remaining very solidly a man and having sexual relationships with a woman, and being very sure that he is not the woman. On the other hand, we find a woman determined to be herself and experience as herself, and to experience a sexual inflow from a man. In the case of the man, as in the case of the woman, we have an unwillingness to be the other sex. This is considered natural but do you know that when this is entirely true, when we have complete determinism to be self and not to be to any slightest degree the other person, there is no sexual pleasure interchange of any kind whatsoever? We get the condition known as Satyrism and Nymphomania. We get a tremendous anxiety to have a sexual flow.

Probably the only reason you can see the universe at all is because you are still willing to be some part of it. Probably the only reason you can talk to people is because you can be the other person you are talking to. Probably the only reason you can really let people talk to you is because you are willing to let the other person be you, somewhat, and he is willing to let you be him to some degree. In view of the fact that space itself is a mock-up, is a state of mind, it can be seen that individuality depends to some degree upon the law that no two things must occupy the same space. When we get this law in action we have a universe. Until this law goes into action there is no universe, and one would be hard put to differentiate entirely. Two things can occupy the same space to the degree that you are willing to believe they can. It is a very easy thing to talk to an audience if you are perfectly willing to be an audience. It is a very difficult thing to talk to an audience if you are unwilling to be an audience. Similarly, it is very difficult to be an audience if you are unwilling to be on the stage. One could conceive that a person who had a considerable amount of stage-fright would be incapable of enjoying a performance of actors. And so it is. We discover the person who is in the audience and has, himself, considerable stage-fright, writhing and feeling embarrassed for every actor who makes the slightest slip or mistake. In other words, we find this person compulsively being on the stage although he is in the audience.

Things of this nature have led more than one philosopher to assume that we were all from the same mould, or that we were all the same thing. This is a very moot question. Processing demonstrates rather adequately that we are all really individuals and that we are not the same individual, and indeed, people who believe we are all the same individual have a very rough time of it. But evidently we could all be the same individual, at least if we were entirely sane.

The physical universe is a sort of hypnotic trance where the individual believes himself to be capable of viewing from various points. The illusion is rendered very excellent by the fact that other individuals believe that they are viewing the same things from the same points as they occupy. We are all, as awareness of awareness units, basically different. We are not the same "pool of Life," and we are all evidently differently endowed, no matter what the Communist Party would like to believe.

One of the most significant differences from man to man is the degree to which he is willing to be Pan-Determined. The man who has to forcefully control everything in his vicinity, including his family, is not being Self-Determined, usually, much less Pan-Determined. He is not being his family. If he were being his family, he would understand why they are doing what they are doing and he would not feel that there was any danger or menace in their going on executing the motions or emanating the emotions which they do. But, anchored down as one person, rather obsessed with the damage that can be done to him or those around him, an individual is apt to launch himself upon a course of heavy, solid, super-control of others. Now let's take the person who is Self-Determined and Pan-Determined in the same situation, and we discover that he would have enough understanding in the vicinity of his family and of his family, and with this understanding would be willing to be and experience as the remainder of the family, and we would find out that he actually could control the family with considerable ease. The oddity of it is that force can control down into entheta—to enturbulation—but that a Pan-Determinism controls upward into greater happiness and understanding since there is more ARC present. You have seen individuals around whom a great deal of peace and quiet obtained. Such individuals quite commonly hold into sanity and cheerfulness many others in their environment who are not basically stable or Self-Determined at all. The individual who is doing this is not doing it out of obsession, he is doing it simply by knowing and being. He understands what people are talking about because he is perfectly willing to be these people. When he falls away from understanding what they are talking about he has also fallen away from being willing to be them. The willingness to understand, the willingness to be are, for our purposes, synonymous.

Now how does this Pan-Determinism tie into communication?

We have seen that difficulties arise on the cycle of communication and on the two-way cycle of communication where origins of communication, answers and acknowledgements were scarce. It must be, then, that the individual becoming aberrated through communication, must have conceived the necessity of another determinism. In other words, one has to fall away from Pan-Determinism to get into any of the traps of communication at all.

It is a very fortunate thing for us that Pan-Determinism exists, otherwise there would be absolutely no way whatsoever out of this maze of mis-communication that a person gets into. The only way out of it would be to have other people come around and do enough talking and go to enough movies, and seek out another Self-Determinism which could communicate and make it communicate until one were sane. However, it doesn't happen to work out in an unlimited sense in this way. The oddity is that it works out in "mock-up." Further, it works out best in mock-up, for in mock-up we introduce the idea of Pan-Determinism.

When we ask somebody to get the idea that somebody else is present, who is not, and then have him make this person give him answers, we discover after a while that some major aberrations have blown out of our preclear. In the first part the preclear is actually remedying the scarcity of answers— or, if these were being processed, origins or acknowledgements—and is so disentangling communication lines. The sense of what he would mock the person up as saying would have nothing to do with it. The communication could be almost pure gibberish as long as it was an answer. This would straighten out the bank to a very marked degree. The other factor which enters into this is Pan-Determinism. We are making the individual actually mock up somebody else and

make somebody else say something. In other words, we are
making our preclear take over the control, the start, change
and stop of another communication medium. And with further test and experiment we discover that we can do this for
all the Dynamics, and when we have done this for all the
Dynamics we have brought our preclear up to a point where
he is willing to monitor communications on all the Dynamics.
And when he is willing to do this, and get origins, answers,
and acknowledgements along all the Dynamics, we find that
we have a very serene person who can do the most remarkable things. Anything you have read concerning the potential
abilities of the Clear, and a lot more, comes true when we
follow this course. So it is a very fortunate thing for us that
Pan-Determinism exists. Otherwise there would be no processing anybody.

Remember, when you are explaining this to people, that it
is *willingness* to control on any and all Dynamics, and that it
is not an obsessive or compulsive control to own, protect, or
hide on any Dynamic. All the ills of Earth come from an
obsession to own, control, protect and hide on other
Dynamics than Self. The true enlightenment of this world
has come from Willingness to *be* along any of the Dynamics.

One of the things which gives truth to Pan-Determinism is
the savageness with which the aberrated attempt to drive an
individual away from anything resembling Pan-Determinism.
This is simply an obsessive action on the part of people to
climb up to Pan-Determinism by force. Pan-Determinism
cannot be climbed by force. The ladder to that height is not
made of pikes and spears, spankings and police forces. It is
made of Understanding, Affinity, Reality and Communication.

CHAPTER XII

THE SIX BASIC PROCESSES

Today's auditor must be conversant with six Basic Processes and must be able to get results with these processes before he can expect to get results with higher levels of auditing.

These six processes form a roadway for more than the auditor. We discover that they compose a tone-scale. This tone-scale is as follows: at its lowest and highest reaches, whether by mimicry, words, or mock-up, we have two-way communication. Next above this, occupying a position from about 1.1 to 1.8 on the Chart of Human Evaluation as given in "Science of Survival," we have Elementary Straightwire. Above this we have, from 1.8 to 2.5, Opening Procedure. Above this, from 2.6 to 3.0, we have Opening Procedure by Duplication. Above this we have Remedy of Havingness, from 3.1 to 3.5, and above this, from 3.6 to 4.0, Spotting Spots in Space.

An auditor, in auditing these six basic processes, becomes sufficiently capable in observing and communicating that he can handle (or, can bring the preclear up to the point where he can handle) the "subjective process" which remedies communication, or the other one which is the "One-Shot Clear."

The problem of psychosis never rightly belonged in Dianetics but it has been solved there. Opening Procedure of 8-C and the Mimicry techniques as given in the PABs resolve psychosis. They resolve it rapidly and care for it adequately, and we have no real worry on that score. The only reason we would enter the field of psychosis at all would be to find out how far South our techniques worked.

CHART OF PROCESSES

Where they are on the ARC Tone Scale

Exteriorized

Spot Spots in Space	4.0
Spot Spots in Space	3.6
Remedy of Havingness	3.5
Remedy of Havingness	3.1
Opening Procedure by Duplication	3.0
Opening Procedure by Duplication	2.6
Opening Procedure 8-C	2.5
Opening Procedure 8-C	1.8
Elementary Straightwire	1.8
Elementary Straightwire	1.1
Two-way Communication	1.0
Two-Way Communication	−8.0
"One-Shot Clear"	4.0
"One-Shot Clear"	2.5

As covered much more fully in "The Creation of Human Ability," available from the Hubbard Scientology Organizations, these Six Basic Processes form the background to all processes. Through them we find two-way communication everywhere. It can be said with honesty that there is no auditing without two-way communication.

The process, Two-way Communication itself, could be sub-divided into verbal and non-verbal processes. The verbal processes would include questions about the present time environment and the preclear's life, interests, and so forth, and would get a direct answer to every question, no matter how long the communication lag was. In other words, a two-way communication would be entered upon so as to actually bring the preclear to talk to the auditor. In the case of people who have great difficulties in this line, we have non-verbal techniques such as Mimicry, wherein the auditor mimics the preclear and persuades the preclear to mimic the auditor. Various processes are used, such as passing a ball back and forth between them, nodding, shaking hands, sitting down, standing up, walking across the room and back and sitting down, all of which are effective.

Much of this book, "Dianetics 55!" is on the subject of two-way communication, and the totality of auditing is bringing a preclear into excellent two-way communication, and it is conceived a little difficult by instructors to relay the "process" called Two-way Communication. However, it is actually simplicity itself, for all that is necessary is to get the preclear to actually volunteer communication and answer the communications volunteered to him. There is always something the preclear will talk about.

Mimicry, particularly when used on psychotics, is a precision subject. Mimicry is not a new process, it is almost as old as psycho-therapy, but it is spotty when used without an intimate knowledge of validation. It can be said that that which one validates comes true. The only force or strength Life has is that which derives directly from the upper echelon of Understanding. When Life gets down to a point where it is incomprehensible it cannot relay any understanding. Understanding this is essential for an auditor. He must realize that he gives power to everything he validates. We made something important out of the engram, and by validating engrams, we actually, where they were audited poorly, gave force and power to engrams. Thus it is with the psychotic. To mimic the strange, peculiar, bizarre and unusual things he does is to give force and strength to those things. It cannot be said with sufficient emphasis that the auditor must *never* mimic the strange, bizarre and unusual manifestations of the psychotic. The only way that the auditor can make mimicry work consistently and continually and rapidly, is by validating what the environment considers the agreed-upon, the usual, the routine, the ordinary. Perhaps the psychotic is twisting his hands madly, and occasionally nodding slightly. The auditor, to mimic him, would not twist his hands, but would nod slightly, since a nod is the agreed-upon manifestation in the environment, not the twisting of hands. If the auditor does this, the preclear will begin to nod more and twist his hands less. If the auditor were to begin to mimic the psychotic by twisting hands, he would discover that the psychotic would probably stop twisting his hands, but would do something else more bizarre. And if the auditor mimics this much more bizarre thing, the psychotic will simply go on to something even wilder or might become entirely motionless, for the one fear the psychotic has is becoming predictable. The psychotic is under the control of entities, demon-circuits. He does have a grain of sanity present, otherwise he would not be able to function at all. Therefore, those things which he does which are sane must be mimicked and so reinforced. If an auditor knows this thoroughly and practises it smartly he will discover that psychotics can be brought into two-way communication and moved immediately into Opening Procedure of 8-C, the proper process for psychotics. 8-C, while not a psychotic process, does work on psychotics. However, in working Opening Procedure of 8-C on the psychotic, the auditor must be very careful not to go beyond part "a" for a long, long time.

From the process known as "Two-way Communication" we move on to the process known as "Elementary Straightwire." Elementary Straightwire has two basic commands. One of these commands is used continually, over, and over, and over, and over, until the communication lag is entirely flat on it and then the other command is used over, and over, and over until the communication lag is entirely flat, at which time it will be discovered that the first command will now give communication lag. And so it is used over, and over, and over, and then the second one is used over, and over, and over. In other words, what we do here is to use this process of Elementary Straightwire with just two commands, continually, one command at a time, flattening each communication lag encountered. While one is doing this, of course, one maintains two-way communication. He acknowledges the fact that the preclear has recalled something and is in general alert to receive from the preclear an originated communication, answer it, and give further orders. The two commands of Elementary Straightwire are: "Give me something you wouldn't mind remembering," "Give me something you wouldn't mind forgetting." This can be varied with : "Tell me something you wouldn't mind remembering," "Tell me something you wouldn't mind forgetting." This Elementary Straightwire is a standard form. If it is varied it should be varied towards simplicity. A simple form of straightwire is "Remember something," over and over, again, and again, and again, and again, and again. Do not use, however, "Forget something," since this is far too rough for the preclear. Another even simpler form is to apply "Remember something" to the Dynamics, such as "Remember a man," "Remember a group." The only error that can be made in Elementary Straightwire is to get too fancy, for one does not believe that an auditor who has advanced this far in auditing would make an error in communication. There is an entire gamut which we call "The next to the last list in Self-Analysis" published in the original edition of "Self-Analysis" which has many times been known to break a person from a neurotic to a sane state. This is: "Can you recall a time that is really real to you?" "Can you recall a time when you were communicating well to someone?" "Can you recall a time when someone was communicating well to you?" "Can you recall a time when you felt Affinity for someone?" "Can you recall a time when someone felt Affinity for you?" By keeping this in the Understanding or Affinity line a case advances more rapidly than if mis-emotion and other factors are addressed.

Opening Procedure of 8-C is one of the most effective and powerful processes ever developed and should be recognized and used as such. The main error which is made in the Opening Procedure of 8-C is not to do it long enough. It takes about 15 hours of Opening Procedure of 8-C in order to bring a person into a completely relaxed and Self-Determined state of mind regarding orders. Opening Procedure of 8-C is a precision process. Step "a" of Opening Procedure of 8-C is "Do you see that object?" the auditor pointing. When the preclear signifies that he does, the auditor says, "Walk over to it." When the preclear has walked over to it, the auditor says, "Touch it." When the preclear does, the auditor says, "Let go," and designates another object—a wall, a lamp—calls it by name or not, and goes through the same procedure once more. It is important that the auditor specifically acknowledge each time the preclear has executed the command given. When the preclear has seen the object, when he has walked over to it, when he has touched it, when he has let go—each time the auditor signifies that he has perceived and does acknowledge this action on the part of the preclear. This Step "a" is used until the preclear does it easily, smoothly, without the slightest variation or introduction of any physical communication lag, and has demonstrated completely that he has no upset feeling about the auditor or objects in the room.

When "a" has been run for a length of time necessary to bring the case up tone, Part "b" is run. Part "b" introduces the idea of decision. It is notable that the "One-Shot Clear" must be very strong on this power of decision. It is also notable that a person in extremely bad condition has no power of decision. The commands of Part "b" are: "Pick a spot in this room," and when the preclear has: "Walk over to it," and when the preclear does: "Put your finger on it," and when the preclear has: "Let go." Each time, the auditor acknowledges the completion of the command by the preclear, signifying "All right," "O.K.," or "Fine," making it very plain that he has noticed and approves of and is acknowledging the preclear in following each specific command. He approves of these one at a time in this fashion. The preclear is run on this until he demonstrates no physical communication lag of any kind in making up his mind what to touch, how to touch it, and so forth.

Part "c" of Opening Procedure of 8-C introduces further decision. It goes as follows: the auditor says, "Pick a spot in this room," and when the preclear has, the auditor says, "Walk over to it." When the preclear does, the auditor says, "Make up your mind when you are going to place your finger on it, and do so." When the preclear has, the auditor says, "Make up your mind when you are going to let go, and let go." The auditor each time acknowledges the completion of one of these orders to the preclear.

In doing Opening Procedure of 8-C the preclear must not be permitted to execute a command before it is given, and a two-way communication must be maintained. As I have said, Opening Procedure of 8-C is a very powerful process. If all auditors knew how to do this Opening Procedure of 8-C and could do this very well, we would right there have psychotherapy licked. But we are not trying to lick psycho-therapy. It has never been a major problem to us. We are trying to bring people a long way further North than psycho-therapy ever dreamed of, and Dianetics and Scientology are not psycho-therapies, they are processes which increase the abilities of people.

Opening Procedure by Duplication has as its goal the separating of time, moment from moment. This is done by getting a preclear to duplicate the same action over and over again with two dissimilar objects. In England this process is called "Book and Bottle," probably because these two familiar objects are the most used in doing Opening Procedure by Duplication.

The first step in Opening Procedure by Duplication is to familiarize the preclear with both objects, as to their reality and his ability to own them. One makes him handle them, and feel them, and acquaint himself with them, makes him describe them as objects he is experiencing in present time, not as something related into the past. A little time spent on this can be quite beneficial.

The auditor then begins what will become to the preclear before he is through with this some of the most hated phrases anyone could conceive, but which, by the time the preclear is finished with this, become just like any other phrases. Many people believe that opening Procedure by Duplication induces hypnosis. This is because in running it hypnotism runs off : the preclear, while the hypnotism is running off, may feel quite hypnotized. It is the exact reverse of hypnotism. Hypnotism is an effort to persuade the individual to do nothing, to sit still, and to accept fully the inflow. Opening Procedure by Duplication contains two-way communication, and indeed does not work unless two-way communication is done with it. The main liability in doing two-way communication on Opening Procedure by Duplication is that the auditor, in introducing two-way communication to it, may stray considerably from the pattern laid down. He must not do this. Although he is maintaining two-way communication he must adhere very sharply to the process. He can make the preclear tell more about them, he can make the preclear describe various things which are manifesting themselves to the preclear; he can be insistent the preclear really knows he has just picked this up, but he must stay with this sequence of auditing commands, and may not vary from them even vaguely. He can interject other conversation, but not other auditing commands, into Opening Procedure by Duplication.

The auditing commands are : "Do you see that book?" says the auditor, pointing. When the preclear signifies that he has, the auditor says, "Walk over to it." When the preclear does, the auditor says, "Pick it up." When the preclear does, the auditor says, "Look at it." When the preclear does (usually he was looking at it but now looks at it more closely) the auditor says, "Give me its colour." When the preclear does, the auditor says, "Give me its weight." When the preclear does, the auditor says, "Give me its temperature." When the preclear has, the auditor says, "Put it back exactly as you found it." This action sequence having been completed, the auditor points to the bottle. "Do you see that bottle?" When the preclear does, the auditor says, "Walk over to it." When the preclear does, the auditor says, "Pick it up." When the preclear has, the auditor says, "Look at it." When the preclear does, the auditor says, "Give me its colour." When the preclear has, the auditor says, "Give me its weight." When the preclear has, the auditor says, "Give me its temperature." When the preclear has, the auditor says, "Put it back exactly as you found it." Then the auditor says, pointing out the book, "Do you see that book?" and so on, back and forth, using this exact sequence of commands. The auditor can interject "Describe it more fully." The auditor can sometimes, but not oftener than once every 15 minutes, point to the book, have the preclear go through the full sequence with the book, and then point to the book again, and have the preclear once more go through the full sequence with the book. This will break down the automatic machinery a preclear is bound to set up to compensate for this process. We want to keep the preclear doing it, not his machines. By asking the preclear to describe the object, or describe its temperature more fully in its proper sequence in these commands, machines are also broken down and the alertness and the awareness of the preclear is increased.

The auditor must not omit letting the preclear give him the preclear's reaction. The preclear will pause, seem to be confused. It is up to the auditor at that moment to say, "What happened?" and to find out what happened, and then to continue with the process, having acknowledged the communication of the preclear. An auditor must never be afraid to let a preclear emanate a communication, and an auditor must never fail to acknowledge the completion of an auditing action, no matter how minute.

The Remedy of Havingness is an extremely effective process for it remedies the ability of the preclear to have or not have at will. Sometimes auditors interpret this process as inflow, only. That is because the physical universe is an inflow universe, and it is all too easy for an auditor to assign to auditing and all other actions inflow characteristics only.

The modus operandi of the Remedy of Havingness is to have the preclear mock up something, pull it in, or mock up something and throw it away. It does not matter what you have him mock up. The item can have significance or not as the case may be. Preclears who are low in tone, if this is run on them — and it should not be — have a tendency to make everything they mock up very significant. It is not the significance, it is the mass that counts. However, to keep the preclear interested, or to assist his mocking up, an auditor may designate specific things, and does so.

It will be found that the acceptance level and expectance level of the preclear very definitely monitor what he mocks up, and what he can pull in and what he can throw away. As covered in the Professional Auditor's Bulletins, acceptance level processes can be combined with the Remedy of Havingness.

The commands of Remedy of Havingness are as follows: "Mock up a (planet, man, brick)." "Make a copy of it." "Make a copy of it." "Make a copy of it." And when the preclear has from five to 15 copies, "Push them all together." "Now pull them in on you." When the preclear has done this for some time, the last command is varied by saying, "Throw them away and have them disappear in the distance." In other words, we have the preclear mock up something, and when he has we have him make a copy of it, make another copy, and another copy, and another copy, one at a time, push them together and pull them in or throw them away.

We keep up this process for some time until we are very
certain that he can actually throw things away or pull them
in on himself at will. This is the Remedy of Havingness.
Remedy of Havingness does not mean stuffing the preclear
with energy. It means remedying his ability to have or not
have energy. Run with particular significances such as
money, women, et cetera, one could remedy specific scarcities
on the part of the preclear. But remember that at first they
may be so scarce that at first he may have to waste a large
quantity of them before he can have one.

On an awareness of awareness unit exteriorized we run
Remedy of Havingness, but a little differently. We say, "Put
up eight anchor points." We describe to him how we want
these put up. We want them put up in such a way as to form
the corners of a cube. In other words, these eight anchor
points are not put in a group in front of or behind the preclear, they are to be distributed around him. When the preclear has done this we say, "Pull them into you." We keep this
up for a long time. We also have the preclear exteriorized
mock up eight anchor points and send them away from him.
A preclear exteriorized can be very unhappy about his lack of
havingness and this last process is used to remedy this upset.

Remedy of Havingness is an exteriorization technique. If it
is run on an individual long enough, say eight or ten hours,
he will probably exteriorize at the end of that time. If you
kept on running it as an exteriorized process, given in the
second part above, he would then have his visio clear up, and
he would finally get into very excellent condition. This is
quite a process. However, remember this process depends
upon the preclear following the auditor's orders. Unless the
auditor has guaranteed this by Opening Procedure of 8-C
and Opening Procedure by Duplication, the chances of the

preclear's actually following his orders (although pretending to do so) are very slim. We discovered in old-time Dianetics that the breakdown was in the preclear failing to follow the auditor's orders. Preclears would pretend to follow an auditor's orders but actually would not.

The process known as Spotting Spots in Space is not to be attempted on somebody who is having a difficult time, and when it is attempted it should be accompanied with Remedy of Havingness. One makes a person spot spots in space for a short time, then remedies Havingness, makes them spot spots in space, then remedies Havingness, then spot spots in space. These two processes, Remedying Havingness and Spot Spots in Space actually belong together, however the preclear eventually emerges up in a higher band where he can spot spots in space without remedying Havingness.

The auditing commands are: "Spot a spot in the space of this room." When the preclear has, the auditor says, "Spot another spot," etc. When the preclear gets well into the process in this fashion we say, "Spot a spot in the space of this room." "Walk over to it," and when he has, "Put your finger on it." When he does, "Let go."

The auditor should ask the preclear when he starts this process if the spot has any mass, colour, temperature, or any other characteristics, or "How big is it?" The auditor asks this to make sure that the preclear is actually spotting a spot, a simple location, not a spot that has a mass, temperature, or characteristics. A location is simply a location, it does not have mass, it does not have colour, it does not have any temperature. When we ask the preclear to spot a spot at first his spots are liable to have mass and temperature. We do not object to this, we simply ask him frequently, once we have discovered that his spots do have this, how his spots are getting along, and we remember, on such a preclear, that we must remedy havingness. Eventually he will move out to a point where he is simply spotting locations.

These are the Six Basic Processes that an auditor must know. They are all of them very powerful processes, and each and any one of them can accomplish the goals which were envisioned in "Dianetics: The Modern Science of Mental Health." The essence of these processes is to do them as given, to do them "purely," all the while maintaining a two-way communication with the preclear. Auditors get into minor variations on this set of processes, but these processes were evolved first from theory by myself, were developed in practice by myself, and were then given to many auditors to do, and many auditors were trained in them, and then these processes were refined and inspected until they represent a very broad agreement, and we have found that these commands, as you have them here, are the best commands which can be used in processing a preclear. The failure of an auditor to duplicate, his unwillingness to duplicate, his upset about duplication in general will quite often lead him up the blind alley of varying a process compulsively or obsessively. When he does he can expect to lessen the results. Auditing to-day, by the experience of a very large number of auditors, is a very severe discipline on the individual. It is not an art, and it never will be an art. It is a precision science. In the old days, all this talk about art and intuition and instinctiveness cost a lot of preclears the benefit of auditing. Auditing in the long ago was tremendously complicated but it was none the less precise. Now that it is very simple it is still very precise.

Amongst these processes an understanding of communication lag and Opening Procedure of 8-C were chosen as the two processes to be taught to a very large area which contained a large number of auditors. This area had been noteworthy, heretofore, for the strange results "obtained" by auditors and the strange techniques which were used in it. A couple of auditors were sent into this area to teach everybody communication lag and Opening Procedure of 8-C. Actually these two auditors were originally from this area. They did so, and several lives have been reported saved to date, and a great many cases have been salvaged, and the entire science is looking up in that particular area simply because the area was taught nothing but communication lag and the Opening Procedure of 8-C and did nothing thereafter but this. Out in the outskirts of this area a couple of auditors varied Opening Procedure by Duplication and were reported to be having very good luck with the variation, but these two auditors were not part of the crew who were taught Opening Procedure of 8-C and communication lag, and the results they are obtaining are very junior to the results obtained by their own fellows very close by.

It could be said that the only real danger in auditing was failure. Auditing is the start, change and stop of aberration, or the creation of ability. Today creation of ability takes prominence to a point where aberration drops out of sight and is forgotten. But the auditor who does not obtain results is demonstrating to himself that he cannot control human aberration and human ability, and a demonstration of his failure to himself is sufficient to make him slightly incapable in handling his own difficulties. Thus it is a tremendously important thing that we have processes which, when used exactly as given, and used with skill, produce uniformly good results on preclears. An auditor using these on preclears gets better, and better, and better, and better even when he doesn't have any auditing himself—a thing which was not the story in 1950. When you can control aberration in others, when you can increase the ability of others, you certainly do not worry about your own. An auditor who has consistent failures will eventually drop back to self-auditing, but these processes will cure even that. Self-auditing, of course, is the manifestation of going around running concepts or processes on one's self. One is doing this because he has been made afraid, through his failure on others, of his ability to control his own engrams, facsimiles, thoughts and concepts, and he seeks to control them through auditing. It is not necessary for an individual to audit himself in order to control his own machinery.

Before anyone should adventure in the direction of testing the "One-Shot-Clear" or doing anything about exteriorizing the awareness of awareness unit and so making a Clear, he should be entirely conversant with these processes. Actually, any of these processes run long enough would probably result in an exteriorization. There are faster ways to achieve an exteriorization than these processes, but these processes are preliminary to them. The preclear who cannot follow the auditor's orders will not sit there and do a subjective—which is to say, an out-of-sight, in his own mind—process without varying it. The trouble with the preclear is that he cannot duplicate, he cannot follow the orders of the auditor, and when the auditor tells him to run a concept or a thought, the preclear probably pays token nod to this and runs entirely something else. A very close E-Meter review of a number of preclears who were not advancing under "subjective processes" disclosed that each and every one of them had never run what the auditor told them to run. They were afraid of obeying the auditor, they were afraid of what the auditor was doing, they were afraid of his skill. Opening Procedure of

8-C remedies this fear and brings the inability and unwilling-ness of the preclear out into the open where it belongs.

In Opening Procedure by Duplication we very often get a preclear "blowing the session" where the auditor has run an insufficient quantity of Opening Procedure of 8-C. When a preclear "blows the session" on Opening Procedure by Duplication, the auditor has missed. He has not run enough Opening Procedure of 8-C. How much is enough Opening Procedure of 8-C? Until the person is in very good condition as homo sapiens.

Remember that whether the command is physical or men-tal, the auditor must observe communication lag. In Opening Procedure of 8-C he simply repeats the process command all the way through, and then again, and again and again and in such a way flattens any lag that shows up. He does not repeat the command on which the preclear got the lag. It is easier to do this way, it is a more orderly process when it is done this way. By very close theory, the actual command on which the preclear lagged should be repeated again, but this is not done.

These are the six basic processes which we must know before we can constitute ourselves auditors. These are the processes which are getting results. These are the processes which are making able men and able women.

These processes can be varied into specific uses where abil-ity is concerned. One of the uses of these, for instance, would be to raise the ability of a pilot to fly a plane, or a person to drive a car, simply by having him approach, touch, and let go of various parts of the object to be controlled. The exact procedure as given above of Opening Procedure is run, except that the object to be controlled is used. Typists have learned to type better, people have learned to drive cars better, and many other abilities have been recovered simply by running 8-C. One could envision a pianist who was getting tired, run-down, or upset by his music, coming into full awareness of it once more simply by running 8-C on his instrument or instruments.

If we wanted to increase the ability of a salesman, it would only be necessary to run any of the above processes in their proper position on the tone scale to increase his ability. Abilities increase, in general, when these are run.

When does one run what process? One should have a copy of the Chart of Human Evaluation from "Science of Survival" and know that chart well in order to understand exactly where one starts. In general practice, however, an auditor simply starts with two-way communication, and when he is getting answers to his questions and is talking rather freely with his preclear he goes into Elementary Straightwire, and from Elementary Straightwire he goes into Opening Procedure of 8-C.

There is a variation on two-way communication. If you have a difficulty in getting a preclear started in two-way communication it is a very easy thing to get him talking on problems, and from problems to run this one, "What problem could you be to yourself?" "What problem could you be to others?" running one and then the other each time until the preclear understood he could be an infinity of problems. Many people are so thoroughly scarce on problems that they will not let any go until they know that they can create problems for themselves. When a case is stalling, he is generally finding it very hard to give up a pet problem because he knows he can't have any more. Of course, all this is basically situated on answers. He can't have any answers so he has to have problems, then from problems he finally gets to a point where he can't even have these.

Anyone desiring to be a good auditor should follow this chapter very closely, should provide himself with a copy of "The Creation of Human Ability," and should also procure "Science of Survival" and study them. The best way to become an auditor is to be trained as an auditor. We have found this so much the case that while we offered an examination to anyone who wished to take it to the grade of Hubbard Certified Auditor, or Hubbard Dianetic Auditor, we never expected them to pass it—for they never had, even though it was on the most simple elements as you see before you. There is no substitute for good training.

CHAPTER XIII

THE PROCESSING OF COMMUNICATION

If you will examine the Six Basic Processes you will discover that they are communication processes. The efficacy of 8-C derives from the fact that it places into the realm of knowingness, communication with the physical universe. The physical universe does not give us back answers, but the Opening Procedure of 8-C remedies to a marked degree the liability of this no-answer situation by making the individual aware of the fact that walls are simply walls, that chairs are chairs, and floors floors, and ceilings ceilings. Opening Procedure by Duplication is processing another facet of communication: Terminals, the *object* (terminal) at Cause interchanging flow with the *object* (terminal) at Effect. Elementary Straightwire is simply a communication with the past, and securing of answers from the past, in other words, using the *past* as a terminal. Havingness, in itself, describes the mass at a terminal, or masses, and Spotting Spots in Space improves the tolerance of an absence of a communication terminal.

These Six Basic Processes, as designed, bring an individual up a gradient scale of tolerance for more and more communication. Once a preclear has been pressed through these he is ready for the direct processing of communication. He is not ready for the direct processing of communication until he has been put through these Six Basic Processes.

The ability of an individual depends upon his ability to

communicate. The first and foremost of mechanical abilities is this communication ability. An individual who cannot communicate with something will become the victim of that something. That which a person withdraws from in this universe becomes, to a marked degree, his master. That which one fears becomes one's master. If an individual were willing to communicate with anything and everything in the entire universe he would then be free in the entire universe. Additionally, he would have an unlimited supply of distances and terminals. A barrier, perforce, is something which an individual cannot communicate beyond. When we see space as a barrier, its total operation as a barrier is the inability of the individual to be at the other extreme end of that space or outside that space. When we see energy as a barrier, we simply see it as something which will not permit the egress or ingress of an individual. When we see mass, walls or time as a barrier, we mean "imagined impossibility of communication." If you do not imagine that you cannot communicate, then there cannot be a barrier.

At the same time we are placed up against this conundrum: in the absence of communication, in the absence of interchanges of communication, in the absence of other terminals, flows, and terminals to which others can communicate, an awareness of awareness unit is not, by its own consideration, living. Livingness is communication. Communication is livingness. We add to this the variant degrees of Affinity. We add to it Agreements and attain Reality, but still these are only significances entered into communication. Any and all types of significances can be entered into communication in order to "give a reason for" communication. These "reasons for" are simply reasons for a game, reasons to have communication.

In the light of the concept of Pan-Determinism we see that an individual has to assume that he cannot know what another is talking about if he wishes to communicate with and depend upon the communications of that other. In other words, he has to pretend he cannot communicate. An individual who has some sort of barrier around him must pretend that he cannot communicate beyond that barrier. Actually this is nothing more nor less than a pretence. These barriers are the shadows through which the fish would not move. They could have swum through these shadows except for the fact that they did not believe they could penetrate beyond the shadows. It could be said that belief alone is the reason for any entrapment.

However, there are the mechanics of entrapment and we discover that an entrapment is a communication barrier. An individual becomes entrapped in something because he does not believe he can communicate outside of it, or he becomes fixated on a terminal *as* a terminal herself.

To be very precise, the reason why an individual is entrapped has to do with scarcity of communication. An individual is still waiting, is still looking towards something, expecting it to communicate to him. It has not, and he has eventually turned his attention slightly off of this onto something else which he expects to communicate to him. And when this does not, he expects communication and so finds it elsewhere, but each time he sets up one of these expectancy lines he is to that tiny degree trapped against the terminal from which he was expecting but did not get communication. Thus, we have the entire bundle known as the reactive mind, the entire anatomy of ridges, and any other enturbulative mechanism, and even problems themselves, being a seemingly endless chain of communication scarcities.

What are the specific scarcities in a communication line? There is no scarcity of silence. Anyone has far too much silence. Silence might be conceived to be the native state of a thetan—an awareness of awareness unit—but it is not, for obviously a thetan is alive only to the degree that he is communicating, is action—concentrated only to the degree that he is living. We discover that the tiny cells of the body consider themselves to be the very mirrors of truth when they are the most silent. There is an interesting and peculiar test here where the auditor has the preclear mock up in any area which contains a somatic a great many answers or originated communications from these "dead cells" and we discover this somatic-ridden area coming to life, waking up, becoming active once more. This in itself is a specific for all types of somatics. All one has to do is to have the preclear mock up answers in these dead cell areas. An ultimate truth, which is studied to a far greater extent in "The Creation of Human Ability", is a Nothingness, but this ultimate truth is not Life. Life is composed of this pretence that one cannot communicate, that one must communicate. It is composed of this intricate tangle of communications and self-erected barriers which give us games. When we get too deeply immersed in this game, when answers get entirely too scarce, we forget that we were the ones who interposed the idea that no answers were to be given.

Silences do not process. There is entirely too much silence on the track. Remember that: it does not process. You can fill silence, but silence itself is death. When you process silence you process the preclear down towards death, not upward towards life. The way to process him upward towards life is by supplying his scarcity of communication. We find the preclears who are in the worst condition are the preclears who are the most silent, the most out of communication. These are the closest to death, closest to aberration. The way to get them alive again is to remedy some of the scarcity of communication. For a preclear who is in very bad shape, or in common practice, any preclear you would encounter, you would use first the Six Basic Steps in order to bring the individual up to something approaching a livable communication strata. And then you would go immediately into the remedy of scarcity of communication by having him mock up himself, even if just as ideas, the various parts of a two-way cycle of communication.

The parts of a communication cycle that have to be remedied are: (1) originated communications, (2) people to communicate to, or other awareness of awareness units to communicate to, (3) answers, (4) acknowledgements, and additionally, but not as important, (5) arrivals, (6) departures.

It is not necessary that the preclear have the ability to mock up or put out and hear back sound. In other words, sonic and visio are not necessary to this process. The entirety necessary is the idea of communication. You might say you have him mock up a "verbalizing idea."

A preclear will sort through, himself, parts (2), (3), (4), (5) and (6) if the preclear is simply told to "mock up some people speaking." He will, in rotation, get people answering, people acknowledging, people greeting him, and people saying goodbye to him. Because the preclear is usually far down the Tone-Scale on origin and ideas, and because "necessity level," other determined forces, have been necessary to get him into communication, it is likely that he will not, himself, spot the origination of communication, and the auditor will have to call his attention to this.

Remember this is not done on a preclear who has not first been put through his paces on the Six Basic Processes, for an auditor sitting there asking the preclear to mock up answers, or acknowledgements, or originated communications could not otherwise be sure that the preclear is doing this at all. Further, the preclear's attention is very likely to stray into various portions of his own bank, for his bank starts to come to pieces under the impact of all these communications.

The preclear must be kept at his job. His mocking up of communications must be kept at a simplicity and out of deep significances, and if his attention seems to fixate upon flows and he begins to "wrestle with mass," the auditor should get him back into mocking up communication as fast as possible.

What degree of originality is required of a preclear in mocking up any of these originative communications, answers, or acknowledgements? The answer to this is "none." No variety is necessary whatsoever. Simply the idea of communication, with some sort of a specific idea being communicated, is all that is necessary. Having the preclear, silent himself, mock up before him something saying "Hello," and saying "Hello" again, and saying "Hello" again, and having him mock this up behind him saying "Hello," and saying "Hello," and saying "Hello," would be quite adequate for an originated communication. Having the preclear mock up any banality such as "All right," or "O.K.," serves very well for both answers and acknowledgements. We are not at all concerned with the significance of the communication. We do not want long and involved communications. The preclear will try to get off into them. He will also try to get into his prenatal bank, his early childhood, and eight lives ago. We do not want him to do this, we want him to go on mocking up originated communications, answers, acknowledgements. We are validating ability, we are not trying to get rid of inabilities in his past. We are trying to increase his ability to communicate in the present, and originate communications, and take a Pan-Determinism of all communicating terminals. We are not trying to get him to run out anything in the past. I know that an old Dianeticist is going to have a very hard time restraining himself from running out the prenatal which immediately appears after the preclear has made something say "Hello" to him 15 or 20 times. It is the auditor's job to make the preclear go on having the preclear or something say "Hello" or "Okay," or "I did it," and to ignore that engram. The number of engrams which will blow into view and beg to be run are countless. The auditor is not interested in these. Of course, if the preclear wants to tell the auditor about these, the auditor must permit the preclear to originate communication and must answer it simply to get the preclear to originate communication. He should not let the preclear go on, and on, and on discussing what has occurred, once the preclear has told him the essentials of it. The auditor wants to get the preclear back onto mocking up originating communications, answers and acknowledgements. The auditor is also making the preclear mock up something to talk to while he is doing this, a point which is cared for automatically and which is not addressed actually and actively in auditing. Naturally, if there is a spot in the air out there saying "Hello," or "Okay," or "I did it," the preclear is assuming that there is something alive there that can say "Hello" to him.

All manner of thinkingness machines, large black masses, white and green fire, purple spheres, falling stars, shooting rockets, may appear in the preclear's bank while he is undergoing this process. The auditor is not interested in this phenomenon, he is merely interested in getting the preclear to mock up further communication.

It does not matter if the preclear says these communications himself aloud or simply does them quietly to himself. The necessity here is not sound. Sound is a by-product of communication. It is the carrier wave of communication and is not itself communication.

Some interesting variations can be worked on this, but they are not advised, and indeed they violate the terms of this process, but they demonstrate how much power this process has. One has the preclear say aloud, "Okay, Mamma," a few hundred times. He will be amazed at the amount of variation which will occur, the communication lags, the impatience, the anger, the amount of data which will jump up about Mamma. But this data that is jumping up is simply the bank which is triggered to agree with what the preclear is doing at this moment. In other words, that is stimulus response. Restimulation is stimulus-response and is covered in great detail in "Dianetics: The Modern Science of Mental Health." We could clear away an ally, we could do almost anything we wanted to do in Book One with this process of remedying the scarcity of communications.

Another point immediately arises, as to whether or not Havingness has to be remedied on the preclear. It has not been found necessary to remedy havingness on the preclear if one is actually remedying the scarcity of communication. This is a great oddity, for the preclear's bank, being composed of tangled and unfinished communication lines, starts to come apart the moment you begin to remedy the scarcity of originated communications, answers, and acknowledgements. Some of these black masses which the preclear has fondly held before his face blow into forever, and yet the preclear does not need his mass remedied. The reason why he had to have mass was to compensate for the lack of communication. Where you have had a lack of communication you are liable to have a mass. As an example of this, an individual loses an ally and then keeps close by him a ring which belonged to that ally. The ring is a substitute communication terminal for the ally. After a while one begins to believe that he really has to have mass; he doesn't have to have mass at all. The remedy of the scarcity of communications cures a person of having to have mass, having to eat obsessively, or do anything else obsessively.

Along with the remedy of originated communications, the preclear's imagination rises quite markedly, and thus he is able to imagine new games and new ways of communication with sufficient rapidity to compensate for the old games which you are taking away from him. Actually the preclear, being a preclear, is a game, perhaps even the last last-ditch game in which the individual could engage.

When the auditor has the preclear run acknowledgements, the wording is: "I did it." This will remedy responsibility difficulties. All automaticity comes about through lack of acknowledgements (absent players, secret players).

In view of the fact that Pan-Determinism is control on all Dynamics, and in view of the fact that control is start, change and stop, one can have the preclear stop making things communicate for a moment, and then change the communication, and then start anew. This gives the preclear practice in starting, changing and stopping.

The auditing command which would go with this is simply, "Mock up some answers," "Mock up some original communications." "Mock up some acknowledgements," with enough guiding talk to give the preclear the idea that you do not want new, startling, difficult action but only the simple placing of communication ideas such as "Hello" in the vicinity of the preclear over, and over, and over, and over.

The exact auditing commands to process communications are: *Originated Communications*: Auditor: "Have somebody out there," (indicating a spot in the air) "start saying 'Hello' to you." The preclear does so, is himself silent. When the process is long run: Auditor: "Start saying 'Hello' to a live spot out there." The preclear aloud, or as himself, does so.

Answers: Auditor: "Have a spot out there start saying 'Okay' to you." The preclear does this many times. Auditor: "Start saying 'Okay' to a spot out there."

Acknowledgements: Auditor: "Have a spot out there start saying 'I did it'." When the preclear has, many, many times: Auditor: "Start saying 'I did it' to a spot out there."

The command that turns on a somatic, repeated often enough, will turn it off.

When in doubt, remedy havingness.

This is the processing of communication directly. Remember that it is done after one has already done the Six Basic Processes. Remember that a two-way communication is maintained with the preclear while it is being done, and remember that the preclear must be audited in full understanding and practice of the Auditor's Code, 1954.

CHAPTER XIV

THE ONE-SHOT CLEAR

The goal of the "One-Shot Clear" has been with us since the earliest days of Dianetics. By "One-shot Clear" we meant one phrase or one action given once, or repeated, which would bring into being the Clear as described in "Dianetics: The Modern Science of Mental Health," Chapter II.

It should be understood by this time that the Clear described in "Dianetics: The Modern Science of Mental Health," Chapter II, is actually the thetan exterior of Scientology. The way to clear somebody is to get him out of the influence of his reactive bank and his analytical machinery. When a person is so cleared, his level of knowingness is sufficient to overcome the need of machinery, and the need of stimulus-response mechanisms as contained in his reactive mind.

Long since we have had a "One-Shot Clear" for 50 per cent of the human race. All we say to the individual is, "Be three feet back of your head." If he is, he orients himself, he knows that he is not his body, he knows he does not have to be up against his reactive mind, he has been gotten out of the trap. Of course, there are many other things which you could do to further increase his ability and orient him in this position, but this is not immediately in our province in Dianetics. When an individual is so exteriorized he also can look over the body and patch up pinched nerves, black areas, rearrange the anchor points which create and hold the space of the body, and so repair a body quite excellently. However, it is not the purpose of exteriorization simply to get a person to square away the machine known as the body.

"Be three feet back of your head" is a strange and interesting combination of words. Evidently this simple combination has not been known before by Man. It is notable that one does not say, "Move three feet back of your head," since an awareness of awareness unit does not move, it appears and disappears from locations.

If one uses this "One-Shot Clear" technique, he should be advised that he must not ask or expect of the newly exteriorized person a number of strange or impossible things. He must not ask him to go chasing around finding things. He must not ask him to prove that he is exteriorized. The individual says so—that's the end of it. In Scientology, of course, on Route 1, as contained in "The Creation of Human Ability," we go on to improve the ability of this exteriorized awareness of awareness unit up to a point we call "Operating Thetan." We do this by running many drills and exercises which improve his perception. However, the process of Answers, or even the Six Basic Processes could be run on the individual after he is exteriorized and his exteriorization will markedly increase, and he will get into even better condition as an exteriorized person. If you were to say "Be three feet back of your head" to somebody, and he was, the next thing to do would be to go into Elementary Straightwire and then into Opening Procedure of 8-C, then Opening Procedure by Duplication, then Remedy of Havingness, then Spotting Spots in Space, and then Answers, or, as the last chapter gives forth, "Remedy of Communication." If you did these things just as given in this book you would have something like a stable Clear. You would pay no attention to the fact that he was Clear. As a matter of fact, if you were to run any of these Six Basic processes long enough, and certainly if you were to run answers for any length of time after you have run these Six Basic Processes, you would have somebody exteriorized. It is a peculiar thing that there is no argument about exteriorization. Any argument which has been in existence was born out of the psychiatrist's observation of "compulsive exteriorization." An individual so detested his body that he stayed outside of it. Psychiatrists have been known to give people electric shocks and other "treatments" to get them to get back inside their bodies. This level of punishment, trying to get a person to accept something under duress, does not work. But then, nothing in psychiatry ever worked, except bank accounts. This "compulsive exteriorization" is a manifestation which we call in Scientology "doing a bunk," in other words, "running away." You will occasionally encounter this, but you will not encounter it if you run the six Basic Processes before you go in for exteriorization.

There is, astonishingly enough, a "One-Shot Clear" for the remaining 50 per cent, even if it has to be repeated many times. I have been developing and testing this for some time, and have kept it back on the shelf against a time when we had enough competent auditors to use the process intelligently.

This is a "One-Shot Clear" technique in that one uses one command and so achieves clearing, and after clearing till the stage of exteriorization has been accomplished, one simply goes on using the same type of command. It is a highly effective process, a very violent process. Theoretically it should work on any level of case. In actual practice psychotic, neurotic cases, or people badly out of communication receive it with considerable difficulty and it is not recommended for them, but it would work on them if it could be communicated to them. (On such people use Opening Procedure of 8-C, only.)

The basis for this process is the observation that the MEST universe is a game. One can have a game and know it. He can be in a game and not know it. The difference is his determinism.

Games require space and havingness. A game requires other players. Games also require skill and knowingness that they are games.

Havingness is the need to have terminals and things to play for and on.

When a game is done the player keeps around tokens. These are hopes the game will start again. When that hope is dead the token, the terminal, is hidden. And it becomes an automaticity—a game going on below the level of knowingness. Truthfully, one never stops playing a game one started. He plays old games in secret—even from himself—while playing or not playing new ones. The only real game one can have is in present time. All others are in the past. Anxiety for a game takes one into the past.

The command is, "Invent a game" and when the preclear has, again, "Invent a game." Then: "Mock up somebody else inventing a game."

Having established the fact that an auditing session is in

progress, and established some slight communication with the preclear, the auditor says, "Invent a game." When the communication lag on this is flat the auditor then uses the command, "Mock up somebody else inventing a game." This is the only phrase he utters, but he of course engages in two-way communication with the preclear when the preclear has something to say to him. An auditor has to be a good auditor in order to use this process. Just because it is a simple "one-command" process is no reason why it will work for an auditor who is not cognizant of the Auditor's Code, cognizant of a two-way communication and has some experience in more basic levels of processing.

We use this process as a remedy for the scarcity of games and we use it in full awareness of the processes involved in two-way communication.

It is a murderous process and requires five or ten hours in rough cases to bring about an understanding of existence.

This is not necessarily a recommended process. It is a workable process, it does function, it is fast, but remember that it has the frailty of the ability of the auditor himself. It has the frailty of failing when a two-way communication is not maintained with the preclear, it will fail if the preclear in volunteering information finds no attention from the auditor, it will fail if the auditor does not acknowledge the fact that the preclear has done this. But, if these things are considered, it will work.

This process can be abused by the preclear. He can wander from it. He can sit there in the auditing chair doing other things, but we depend upon the skill of the auditor to see that the preclear is not doing other things, and that he is actually doing the process.

The preclear will "pick his bank clean" rather than invent, he will have doubts that he *is* inventing. But we persevere— and we win.

CHAPTER XV

ARC PROCESSING

If we examine communication we will discover that all communication lag is the introduction of Matter, Energy, Space and Time into communication. The more has been introduced into communication, the less communication there is.

As an example of this let us say that a star in some other galaxy explodes, and then let us trace the length of time necessary for a small amount of that explosion's particles to reach earth across great space. Almost countless light-years elapse before this communication line has been completed. This is a very, very long communication. Not necessarily a communication lag since the progress of the particles is not interrupted. There are no VIAs. Actually, MEST itself does not have a communication lag, it is totally a communication lag.

The more this sort of thing enters into communication, the worse off is the preclear. Thus we can see that the subject

As we examine barriers, we find that they are Matter, Energy, Space and Time. We discover that we can overcome the barriers of Matter, we can climb walls or go through them. We can somehow or other brave or get on the other side of energy barriers. We discover that even space has its

limitations even when it appears as limitless as the space of
this universe (and the space of this universe appears as big as
a person supposes it is big, whereas actually it is, to a thetan
who can get outside of it, about the size of a matchbox to a
child). The one barrier which we discover difficult to get
around is Time.

The basic definition and understanding of Matter, Energy,
Space and Time are not particularly germane in this place.
They are taken up on a much higher theoretical level in
Scientology, but the essence of time is that it is measured or
marked by the motion of particles in space. Space and energy
particles are necessary to have mechanical time, but what is
time, basically? Time is actually consideration. There is
time because one considers there is time.

You must examine the physical universe very closely to
discover that the reason it is always here is because it is, each
particle of it, each cubic inch of space of it, in *forever*. The
physical universe is not moving through time, it is stuck in
time. Each and every part of it is fixed in a *now* which lasts
forever. The only real changes which take place in the physical universe are those introduced into it by Life. We can
argue about this if we want to but we are interested here in
a concept which leads towards a workable process.

We discover that time exists for the individual to the
degree that the individual makes time. Time is an other-
determined thing to nearly everyone alive. He depends on
clocks, he depends on the rising and setting of the sun, he
depends on all manner of mechanisms to tell him what is
time. Actually the more a person is told what time is, the
more he gets into a dependency upon some other consideration, and so he drops into forever. When he stops considering

that he is making time, when he stops making time by considerations, he is dropping himself into a foreverness. He has less and less motion, he has less and less determinism. Time is a very insidious barrier because its apparency would tell an individual that time is created by the movement of things. Actually it is not, it is created by a consideration that things are moving.

The remedy of the barrier of time produces an astonishing effect upon a preclear. When the auditor is auditing one of these two "One-Shot Clear" commands (the one given in the last chapter and the one given in this chapter) he will stumble across quite a bit of complication on the subject of time. An individual told to have some complications by decision will eventually move out into the fact that the most complicated thing he can get into is time, and so this is a very satisfactory game. We can process this factor directly.

This process is the essence of simplicity. It has one command. The command is "Make some time." This is all the command there is. One does not advise or teach the preclear how to make some time. One accepts whatever the preclear decides makes time as the answer. One maintains the two-way communication with the preclear, and answers comments which the preclear has on it. One carefully does not evaluate for the preclear and tell him how to make some time. One does not set an example in making time. One simply has the preclear make some time.

This process on some cases has to be run many hours before the preclear comes into partial control of the barrier of time. When he does this he of course comes into some control of his engram bank and his considerations.

The making of time naturally puts into motion all those silent or motionless masses which are hanging to the preclear and which actually pin together his reactive bank.

This is an enormous joke upon the preclear himself and the universe that he makes all the time he will ever perceive. He cannot possibly get out of phase with "forever" if he is in contact with the foreverness of the space and energy masses of which this universe is composed. When he starts to protest against the universe at large he starts to protest against the foreverness which includes all time, and so he withdraws into earlier times when he was making time in order to have some time himself.

"Make some time," is a process of astonishing ramifications.

But remember, time is a barrier. One could also say, "Make some space," "Make some energy," "Make some objects," "Make some terminals," and have gains in a preclear. But these are barriers. Although a game requires barriers, the preclear already has too many in the past, too few in the present.

Barriers are not life.

We must use three cardinal rules in processing : (1) Process towards truth; (2) Process towards ability; (3) Process towards life.

Auditing commands must emphasize truth, ability, life.

Don't process towards entheta, chronic somatics, difficulties. Ignore them.

The only thing wrong with the preclear is that his attention is fixed on barriers—MEST. His freedom depends upon putting his attention on freedom or present time. Here are two auditing commands. Which is correct? (1) "Find some things you can't do." (2) "Find some things you can do."

The second is correct. The first will almost spin a preclear. Why? Because it concentrates on a lie. A preclear can do anything!

A preclear has a bad leg. Which is the right process? (1) "Touch the back of your chair." (2) "Recall a time when somebody hurt his leg."

The first is correct. It is *faster*. Why? Because it processes towards ability.

We have a preclear who is apathetic. Which process is the right one? (1) "Who used to have headaches?" or (2) "Feel the floor beneath your feet." The second is correct because it processes towards life, not illness.

That which the auditor concentrates upon in auditing comes true. Hence, the processing of MEST gives us new barriers. The processing of life gives new life.

Processing barriers gives us *limited* processes. Processing life gives us unlimited processes. Life is composed of Affinity, Reality, Communication. These make understanding. Modern ARC processing processes communication as given earlier in this volume. ARC processing includes the following powerful processes: (1) "Tell me something you might communicate with." "Tell me something that would communicate with you." (2) "What might you agree with?" "What might agree with you?" (3) "Tell me something you could like." "Tell me something that might like you." These are present time, not past or future processes. They produce very strong reactions. They solve *very* rough cases. They are summed up in a simple process which does not dispense with them: "Tell me something (someone) you could understand." "Tell me something (someone) who could understand you."

Note - Of course a very basic process which resolves chronic somatics, eye difficulties, any specific item is to have the affected part or bad area of energy say "hello" and "okay" and "all right" until it is in good condition — not that an auditor should address specific conditions — LR

CHAPTER XVI

EXTERIORIZATION

The auditor will be confronted with a great many problems in exteriorization once he has exteriorized his preclear. The things not to do and to do are as follows:

(1) Do not require the awareness of awareness unit to again put its attention on the body.

(2) Do not make the person prove that he is exteriorized.

(3) Do not make the newly exteriorized person discover, find things, read the future, or do other nonsensical tricks.

(4) Maintain the Auditor's Code more severely than before.

(5) Continue the process on which the preclear exteriorized.

If the auditor knows these things he will not get the preclear and himself into trouble. The auditing command "Be three feet back of your head" sometimes gets the auditor into more trouble than he is equipped to handle. The preclear may do a compulsive exteriorization, "do a bunk," and drop his body limp in the chair and give from that body no sign that he is hearing any of the auditing commands given by the auditor. One such case was pleaded with for half an hour by an auditor along the lines that the preclear should remember her husband, should think of her children, should come back and live for the sake of her friends, and found no response from the preclear. Finally the auditor said, "Think of your poor auditor," at which moment the preclear promptly returned.

A limited "compulsive exteriorization" is the preclear going out of the body and getting plastered against the ceiling, or falling in terror upward into the sky (an inverting of gravity). This manifestation is equally upsetting.

If a preclear has been given the command "Be three feet back of your head" and if he "does a bunk," or if he "falls out of his body upward," all the auditor has to do is to get into a two-way communication with the preclear. Actually, he should have, as an auditor, an excellent command of the Chart of Human Evaluation and "Science of Survival." He would not then tell a preclear below 2.0 on the Tone Scale to "Be three feet back of your head," for when they do, at these lower levels of the Tone Scale, it is on a compulsive or obsessive level, and all the preclear can think of is to try and get away.

Another remedy, if this untoward and strange occurrence happens, is to ask the preclear to "Reach from your position to your body," "Withdraw from the body," "Reach for the body," "Withdraw from the body" or "Decide to run away and run away," several times. Remember, such things as this occur only when the auditor has not placed his preclear on the Tone Scale before he began to audit him.

The way to get away from these entirely is to audit the Six Basic Processes on the preclear, and then audit either or both of the "One-Shot Clear" processes of Remedying Communication and Time Processing until the preclear exteriorizes and then simply go right on auditing the process which exteriorized the preclear. Remember that a preclear exteriorized is simply an awareness of awareness unit which has been taken out of a trap, and the awareness of awareness unit had not changed any from the basic individual, but now recognizes itself to be out of the trap and is quite happy about it.

A very funny manifestation occurs on some very low-toned preclears when they talk about exteriorization. They say, "I'm over *there*." This, of course, is impossible. An individual is always *here*. It is here where you are. Lord knows what this individual who says "I'm over there" has exteriorized—a circuit, a mock-up, some such thing. He himself definitely is not. Another manifestation we have is "buttered all over the universe." A preclear who is buttered all over the universe is one who does not know where he is and if we ask him many, many times, over and over and over, each time making him get a spot with certainty, "Can you find a spot where you are not?" we will gradually narrow down his area. What has actually happened in such a case is that the preclear has used remote viewpoints, and has left remote viewpoints located all over everywhere to such a degree that the preclear thinks he is any place rather than where he is.

The main thing one has to know about exteriorization is that it takes place. If one uses the Six Basic Processes, remembers the Auditor's Code, and the two "One-Shot Clear" processes, he is then quite safe on exteriorization, for it will occur when it occurs, and the thing to do after it occurs is to do the same process one was doing when it did occur. Of course, one should acknowledge the fact of the preclear's mentioning it and one should certainly permit the preclear to discuss it, but

one should continue with the process which exteriorized him,
unless, of course, one is very well trained in exteriorization
exercises.

As exteriorization drilling, as an activity, is most germane
to the realm of Scientology, further knowledge of it and
about it is written up in "The Creation of Human Ability."
Here are given the Route 1 steps which should be run after
an exteriorization takes place.

The creation of a Clear undertaken in 1950 actually was
this manifestation of exteriorization happening at some ran-
dom moment and not being adequately cared for after it
occurred. Nobody remarked upon the fact that he was a
distance from the body because most of the people who were
thus exteriorized had very good visio on their own banks but
very poor visio on the immediate environment. A little more
exteriorization work and any one of these Clears would have
suddenly found himself out in the room looking at the room
directly without the aid of his eyes.

We wanted Clears in 1950. We still want Clears. We now
have the way to make them, the way to make them stable,
and the way to make anybody you process far more able.

The by-word on this is not to address specific errors or
difficulties, but to validate abilities and process immediately
towards the acquisition of further and higher abilities. We are
not in there to pay attention to all of the bad things in the
world, since these are composed only of the imaginings of the
individual. Let us increase the ability of the individual to
create, to be, to perceive, and increase his ability to associate
all along the dynamics. If we could do this it would be a far,
far better world.

GLOSSARY

ALLY : A person from whom sympathy came when the preclear was ill or injured. If the ally came to preclear's defense or his words and/or actions were aligned with the preclear's survival, the reactive mind gives that ally the status of always being right—especially if this ally was obtained during a highly painful engram.

AS-IS (verb) : To view anything as it is, without any distortions or lies; to duplicate; to perform an as-isness. The general rule of auditing is that anything which is unwanted and yet persists must be thoroughly viewed (perfect duplication), at which time it will vanish. If only partially viewed, its intensity, at least, will decrease. (*Ref.:* Scientology Axiom 30, and Axiom 11, which gives the four conditions of existence, of which as-isness is one. See *Scientoloty 0—8: The Book of Basics* by L. Ron Hubbard.

AUDITING : Processing.

AUDITOR : A person trained and qualified in applying Dianetics and/or Scientology processes and procedures to individuals for their betterment; called an auditor because auditor means "one who listens".

AWARENESS OF AWARENESS UNIT : Thetan.

BANK : Reactive bank; reactive mind.

CHRONIC SOMATIC : A somatic of long duration.

CIRCUITS : Reactive patterns; apparent personalities or communications which are in actuality only engramic content. Word derives by analogy from electronic technology. (See also Demon-circuits.)

CLEAR (noun) : Term originated in Dianetics by analogy to an adding machine from which old answers have been cleared (by pushing button marked "Clear") so that new sensible answers can be obtained. A being able to be at cause over mental matter, energy, space and time as regards the First Dynamic (survival for self).

DEMON-CIRCUITS : Stimulus-response mechanisms in the bank which mirror the personalities of persons antipathetic to the preclear and which act very much as if they were actual personalities; entities.

ENTITIES : Demon-circuits and similar phenomena.

ENGRAM : A specialized kind of facsimile which differs from other mental image pictures in that it contains as part of its content unconsciousness and physical pain.

ENTHETA : From "enturbulated theta"; especially, destructive communications.

FACSIMILES : Mental energy pictures, mental image pictures, but distinct from *mock-ups*; the contents of the reactive mind; continuously made recordings in mental picture form, unknowingly created by the individual of his perceptions of the environment, done by an involuntary intention not within the individual's awareness or control.

LOCK : Mental image picture of a non-painful but disturbing experience, the force of which is derived from an earlier engram and secondary which the experience has restimulated.

MOCK-UP (noun) : A knowingly created mental model, construction or picture. (Distinct from facsimile.) MOCK UP (verb) : To produce a mock-up.

"ONE-SHOT CLEAR" : Thetan exterior, when accomplished by a single ("one-shot") command.

PRECLEAR : Pre Clear; a person not yet Clear, or a person being audited, who is thus on the road to Clear.

PROCESS : A question or set of questions or directions used by an auditor in a session to help a person find out things about himself and life. The many processes in Scientology technology are used on a precise gradient which leads the person at each level easily to a specific major gain in freedom and ability.

PROCESSING : Auditing; the application of Dianetics and/or Scientology technology to individuals for their betterment.

REACTIVE MIND : Reactive bank; composed of *engrams, secondaries* and *locks,* the reactive mind can be described as a collection of facsimiles (recordings in mental energy picture form) made and retained unknowingly by the individual of the universe around him, which are not under his volitional control and which exert force and the power of command over his awareness, purposes, thoughts, body and actions. Resolved by processing, using standard Dianetics and Scientology.

RESTIMULATION : Mechanism whereby the environment reactivates a facsimile, which then acts back against the body or awareness of awareness unit.

RESTIMULATOR : Any part of the environment sufficiently similar to a facsimile in the reactive bank (specifically, in an engram, secondary or lock) to bring that part of the bank into confusion with present time ("drawn out of the files"), producing stimulus-response behavior in the individual.

SECONDARY : Orig. "secondary engram"; a mental image picture of a moment of severe and shocking loss or threat of loss which contains misemotion (anger, fear, grief, apathy, etc.). It is called a secondary because its force depends upon an earlier engram, which holds it in place.

SOMATIC : Noun taken from adjective, somatic—bodily; means essentially any body sensation, illness, pain or discomfort; especially, those stemming from the reactive mind.

THETAN : From Theta (Life Static), a word taken from the Greek letter θ, *theta,* tradition symbol for thought or spirit. The thetan is the individual himself—not the body, the mind, etc.; it is that which is aware of being aware; awareness of awareness unit.

THETAN EXTERIOR : An awareness of awareness unit able knowingly to be at a distance from the body.

TONE-SCALE : A gradation of the various factors of behavior, thought, emotion, communication, etc., plotted on a precise scale of levels of survival potential; ARC Scale. (See especially "Science of Survival" by L. Ron Hubbard.)

DIANETICS IS HERE!

Through extensive research in Dianetic technology, L. Ron Hubbard has recently made several astounding breakthroughs.

This technology is now available to you. NEW ERA DIANETICS is for everyone. Learn the true magnitude of the gains that lie in store for you with NEW ERA DIANETICS! Contact your nearest Church of Scientology and ask for the Registrar!

CONTACT YOUR NEAREST
SCIENTOLOGY ORGANIZATION

UNITED STATES

ADVANCED ORGANIZATION

Church of Scientology
Advanced Organization
of Los Angeles (AOLA)
1306 N. Berendo Street
Los Angeles, California 90027

SAINT HILL ORGANIZATION

Church of Scientology
American Saint Hill
Organization (ASHO)
1413 N. Berendo Street
Los Angeles, California 90027

PUBLICATIONS ORGANIZATION

Church of Scientology
Publications Organization U.S.
4833 Fountain avenue,
East Annex
Los Angeles, California 90029

LOCAL CHURCHES

AUSTIN
Church of Scientology
2804 Rio Grande
Austin, Texas 78705

BOSTON
Church of Scientology
448 Beacon Street
Boston, Massachusetts 02215

BUFFALO
Church of Scientology
1116 Elmwood Avenue
Buffalo, New York 14222

CHICAGO
Church of Scientology
839 Chicago Avenue
Evanston, Illinois 60202

DENVER
Church of Scientology
375 S. Navajo
Denver, Colorado 80223

DETROIT
Church of Scientology
3905 Rochester Road
Royal Oak, Michigan 48067

HONOLULU
Church of Scientology
143 Nenue Street
Honolulu, Hawaii 96821

LAS VEGAS
Church of Scientology
846 E. Sahara
Las Vegas, Nevada 89104

LOS ANGELES
Church of Scientology
4810 Sunset Boulevard
Los Angeles, California 90027

Church of Scientology
Celebrity Centre Los Angeles
1551 N. La Brea
Hollywood, California 90028

MIAMI
Church of Scientology
120 Giralda
Coral Gables, Florida 33134

NEW YORK
Church of Scientology
28-30 West 74th Street
New York, New York 10023

PHILADELPHIA
Church of Scientology
8 West Lancaster Avenue
Ardmore, Pennsylvania 19003

PHOENIX
Church of Scientology
908 E. Camelback Road
Phoenix, Arizona 85014

PORTLAND
Church of Scientology
333 South West Park Avenue
Portland, Oregon 97205

SACRAMENTO
Church of Scientology
825 15th Street
Sacramento, California 95814

SAN DIEGO
Church of Scientology
348 Olive Street
San Diego, California 92103

SAN FRANCISCO
Church of Scientology
83 MacAllister
San Francisco, California 94102

SEATTLE
Church of Scientology
1318 2nd Avenue
Seattle, Washington 98101

ST. LOUIS
Church of Scientology
3730 Lindell Boulevard
St. Louis, Missouri 63108

TWIN CITIES
Church of Scientology
2708 E. Lake Street
Minneapolis, Minnesota 55406

WASHINGTON, D.C.
Founding Church
of Scientology
2125 "S" Street, N.W.
Washington, D.C. 20008

CANADA

LOCAL CHURCHES

MONTREAL
Church of Scientology
15 Notre Dame Ouest
Montreal, Quebec H2Y 1B5

OTTAWA
Church of Scientology
124 O'Connor St., 4th Floor
Ottawa, Ontario K1P 5M9

TORONTO
Church of Scientology
385 Yonge Street
Toronto, Ontario M5R 2H5

VANCOUVER
Church of Scientology
1130 Granville Street
Vancouver 10,
British Columbia V6V 1M1

MEXICO

Instituto de Filosofia Aplicada
Havre N°. 32, Col. Juarez
Mexico 6, D.F. Mexico

UNITED KINGDOM

ADVANCED ORGANIZATION/ SAINT HILL

Hubbard College
of Scientology
Advanced Organization
Saint Hill (AOSH UK)
Saint Hill Manor
East Grinstead, Sussex
RH19 4JY
England

LOCAL CHURCHES

EAST GRINSTEAD
Saint Hill Foundation
Saint Hill Manor
East Grinstead, Sussex,
RH19 4JY
England

LONDON
Hubbard Scientology
Organization
68 Tottenham Court Road
London W.1, England

MANCHESTER
Hubbard Scientology
Organization
48 Faulkner Street
Manchester M1 4FH, England

PLYMOUTH
Hubbard Scientology
Organization
39 Portland Square
Sherwell, Plymouth
Devon, England PL4 6DJ

EDINBURGH
Hubbard Academy
of Personal Independence
Fleet House
20 South Bridge
Edinburgh, Scotland EH1 1LL

EUROPE

ADVANCED ORGANIZATION

Church of Scientology
Advanced Organization
Europe
Jernbanegade 6
1608 Copenhagen V, Denmark

SAINT HILL ORGANIZATION

Church of Scientology
Saint Hill Europe
Jernbanegade 6
1608 Copenhagen V, Denmark

PUBLICATIONS ORGANIZATION

Scientology Publications
Organization Denmark
Store Kongensgade 55,
1264 Copenhagen K, Denmark

LOCAL CHURCHES

AMSTERDAM
Church of Scientology
Nieuwe Zijds Voorburgwal 312
1012RV Amsterdam, Holland

AUSTRIA
Scientology Osterreich
Mariahilferstrasse 88a
11 Unterteil,
A-1010 Vienna, Austria

BERN
Church of Scientology
2 Sudbahnhofstrasser
3007 Bern, Switzerland

COPENHAGEN
Scientology Kirken, Danmark
Vesterbrogade 23A-25
1620 Copenhagen V, Denmark

Scientology Kirken,
Copenhagen
Frederiksborgvej 5
2400 Copenhagen NV,
Denmark

GÖTEBORG
Church of Scientology
Küngsgatan 23,
S-411 19 Göteborg, Sweden

MALMÖ
Church of Scientology
Stortorget 27-29,
S-211 34 Malmö, Sweden

MILANO
Hubbard Dianetics Institute
Galleria del Corso 4
20100 Milano, Italy

MUNICH
Church of Scientology
8000 Munchen 2
Lindwurmstrasse 29
Munich, West Germany

PARIS
Church of Scientology
12 Rue de la Montagne
Ste. Genevieve 75005
Paris, France

STOCKHOLM
Church of Scientology
Kammakaregatan 46
S-111 60 Stockholm, Sweden

SOUTH AFRICA

LOCAL CHURCHES

BULAWAYO
Church of Scientology
210-211 Kirrie Bldgs.
Cnr. Abercorn & 9th Avenue
Bulawayo, Rhodesia

CAPETOWN
Church of Scientology
3rd Floor Garmour House
127 Plein Street
Capetown, South Africa 8001

DURBAN
Church of Scientology
57 College Lane
Durban, South Africa 4001

JOHANNESBURG
Church of Scientology
99 Polly Street
Johannesburg, South Africa
2001

PORT ELIZABETH
Church of Scientology
2 St. Christopher's
27 West Bourne Road
Port Elizabeth, South Africa
6001

PRETORIA
Church of Scientology
224 Central House
Cnr. Central & Pretora Streets
Pretoris, South Africa 0002

AUSTRALIA/
NEW ZEALAND

LOCAL CHURCHES

ADELAIDE
Church of Scientology
28 Weymouth Street
Adelaide, SA 5000, Australia

MELBOURNE
Church of the New Faith
724 Inkerman Road
North Caulfield 3161
Melbourne, Victoria, Australia

PERTH
Church of Scientology
Pastoral House
156 St. George's Terrace
Perth 6000, Western Australia

SYDNEY
Church of Scientology
1 Lee Street
Sydney 2000
New South Wales, Australia

AUCKLAND
Church of Scientology
New Imperial Buildings
44 Queen Street
Auckland 1, New Zealand